... ...e cornerstone of result-based ...
... ...is new book and use it'

> Tim Ferriss, bestselling author of
> *The 4-Hour Work Week*

'All the strands of Koch's uniquely powerful thinking poured into one volume. Packed with counterintuitive advice, this is the rare business book that can genuinely transform your life and work prospects. It's already given me a stack of invaluable ideas'

> Tom Butler-Bowdon, author of
> *Never Too Late To Be Great*

'Simple ideas that can turn your business and your life around. I highly recommend it'

> Al Ries, author of *War in the Boardroom*

'It's time for managers to stop wasting time on bureaucracy and start working on the few things that count to create value. This book shows precisely how'

> Jim Lawrence, CEO,
> Rothschild North America

'Richard Koch sees so clearly that good management and leadership come from within, and that liberating talent in yourself and in others is the key to success. This is a must-read book for anyone who wants to be a great leader and achieve extraordinary results'

> Rt Hon Lord Smith of Finsbury, Chairman, Environment
> ...ency

'A great book, completely different from *The 80/20 Principle*, written exclusively for managers, and intensely practical'

Professor Andrew Campbell, Director,
Ashridge Strategic Management Centre

'I have long felt that laziness is a good quality in a manager without knowing either why or how to practise it as much as I would have liked. Richard's new book explains both why and how. I wish it had been published long ago'

Colin Drummond OBE, Chief Executive, Viridor

'The good thing about this book is that it makes you think. The bad thing is that it doesn't let you off the hook. But at least Richard Koch offers managers ten ways you can achieve extraordinary outcomes. Some of the ten will surprise you'

Christopher Outram, Co-Founder & Chairman Emeritus,
OC&C Strategy Consultants

'Richard Koch offers tremendous insight and practical guidance to help managers focus on the vital few things in their jobs, so that they can surf their objectives and achieve more with less'

Dr Peter Johnson, Fellow, Exeter College, Oxford University

'Koch provides a step-by-step guide to greater efficiency, helping readers with topics including mentoring, leveraging influence, finding meaning and direction, developing strategy and consistently pursuing the biggest goals with the smallest effort . . . This easy-to-follow, substantive work helps readers develop a managerial style that's truly worthwhile'

Publishers Weekly

THE

80

20

MANAGER

About the Author

Richard Koch is the bestselling author of *The 80/20 Principle*, which has sold over a million copies and been published in thirty-one languages. He is also a highly successful entrepreneur and investor, whose ventures have included Filofax, Plymouth Gin, Belgo and Betfair. He was formerly a partner of Bain & Company and co-founder of LEK Consulting. He is British and lives in Gibraltar.

To find out more about Richard and his work, visit www.richardkoch.net.

THE

80
20
MANAGER

RICHARD KOCH

piatkus

For Nicholas Walt, with belated thanks

PIATKUS

First published in Great Britain in 2013 by Piatkus
This paperback edition published in 2015 by Piatkus

Copyright © Richard Koch 2013

3 5 7 9 10 8 6 4 2

A CIP catalogue record for this book
is available from the British Library.

ISBN 978-0-7499-5926-5

Typeset in Janson Text by Palimpsest Book Production Ltd, Falkirk, Stirlingshire
Printed and bound in Great Britain by Clays Ltd, St Ives plc

Papers used by Piatkus are from well-managed forests
and other responsible sources.

MIX
Paper from
responsible sources
FSC
www.fsc.org   FSC® C104740

Piatkus
An imprint of
Little, Brown Book Group
Carmelite House
50 Victoria Embankment
London EC4Y 0DZ

An Hachette UK Company
www.hachette.co.uk

www.piatkus.co.uk

As to methods there may be a million and
then some, but principles are few.
The man who grasps principles can
successfully select his own methods.
The man who tries methods, ignoring
principles, is sure to have trouble.

Ralph Waldo Emerson

Acknowledgements

This book would not have existed without Matthew Kelly, who generously wrote to me suggesting the idea some two years ago. He has been invaluable throughout the process, particularly in the chapter on Mentoring and in the Foreword he provided, and in commenting on drafts of the book as they emerged. Thank you, Matthew.

Next, I want to give full credit to the managers who have supplied me with several of the book's lessons. Many of them are cloaked in modest anonymity, but I would like to thank in particular Raymond Ackerman, Antony Ball, Bill Bain, the late Bruce Henderson, Alex Johnson, Jamie Reeve, and Egon Zehnder – all have been a source of great inspiration to me.

Deep appreciation goes to the friends who have read parts of the manuscript or supplied important ideas to the book, in particular to David Collis and Greg Lockwood, as well as to some of the people already named.

To Nicholas Walt, I give belated but extremely heartfelt appreciation (see Way Two).

Everyone at my publishers, Piatkus and Little, Brown, has been wonderfully enthusiastic about the project and performed where it matters. I am grateful in particular to Tim Whiting, Zoe Goodkin, Philip Parr, Kate Hibbert, Maddie Mogford, Carleen Peters and Jo Wickham.

As always, my agent Sally Holloway has been a wonderful co-conspirator throughout the process and kept me continually excited about it.

I also want to thank my assistants, Francisco Martins, and Doug Blowers, for their support in so many different ways.

Finally, Matthew and Tocker have kept me sane and suitably distracted throughout the book's writing, and I love you both.

Contents

Foreword

A little over a year ago I was reading *The 80/20 Principle* for about the tenth time. I happened to be working with managers from several of the world's largest companies and was stunned by how little they applied the principle to the way they managed. In conversations it became clear that they knew the 80/20 Principle, but the way they managed demonstrated that they weren't deploying its practical power in their daily work.

So I wrote to Richard and suggested he write the book you are holding in your hands now.

Why did I do that?

Because I want to see more 80/20 managers in the world. Lots more.

What does that mean?

I want more executives who achieve great results, transform their companies, and help the people they lead to do their best work; and at the same time to feel more fully alive, satisfied and happy themselves. Most of all, I want to see the very character of the way we do business transformed, so everyone realizes that extraordinary results are possible with ordinary effort – if we really care about achieving those results.

The virtue of this book is that it is immensely practical. You will start applying the lessons as soon as you read them. Are you ready to take your life and your business to the next level?

The genius of the 80/20 Principle is that it is counter-intuitive. The genius of Richard Koch is that he makes the counter-intuitive accessible.

At the same time it is essential to understand that while Richard makes high achievement as easy as it can be, it's not true that you can attain great goals without some unusual effort. The point is that this unusual effort doesn't have to be a grind. It doesn't have to be soul-destroying. It doesn't have to compromise your values. It doesn't have to risk overwhelming you or your loved ones. In fact, all of these things would be clear signals that you were on the wrong path.

The unusual effort that this book so brilliantly encourages is in the mind. Are you willing to *think* in a new way, on a new level? If so, prepare yourself to sit at the feet of one of the masters. He is about to teach you how to use the most productive levers at your disposal, including many you thought were out of your reach.

If you put into practice what you learn within these pages, you will find that it is the most enjoyable effort you have ever exerted, not only for you but for everyone around you. When correctly embraced, the 80/20 Principle is life-enhancing for everyone.

I have enjoyed watching this book evolve, and it has been a privilege to watch Richard work, see his ideas develop, and observe his passion for helping you, the reader. This is a book that will help you become the best version of yourself; and it will lead you to help everyone else live their best life, too.

Read this book and you will enjoy it. Live this book and you will find it is a game-changer.

Everybody wants to work for an 80/20 manager.

Isn't it time you became one?

Matthew Kelly
Singer Island, Florida
June 2012

Preface

When work is a pleasure, life is a joy!
When work is a duty, life is slavery.
The Lower Depths, Maxim Gorky

Would you like to simplify your work and life? Is the sheer volume of work you face so daunting that you often fall behind? Does it seem that work controls you, rather than the other way round?

If so, you're not alone. A large number of managers – especially in these difficult times – feel like that.

But there is a solution. And that solution will not only improve your performance exponentially but will enable you to do so by working *less* hard.

Yes, really.

The answer is to become a much more *effective* manager, and this book will show you how. It will also show how to enjoy your work and build a fulfilling career without stress or long hours. And how to achieve far more than you do at the moment without denying who you are, or short-changing your family and friends.

How is all of this possible?

Most companies, and certainly most managers, focus on inputs rather than outputs. They look at process – the 1001 tasks you have to do each week. Whereas they should be looking at results – specifically at what produces the *best* results. Yet, as this book will show, when you really scrutinize what produces great results, the answer is surprising.

As you will discover, most great results are achieved through relatively little action and energy. But the small inputs that produce big results are generally hidden by a mass of inputs that produce a few good results, and often many bad ones. Companies and managers tend to look at averages, not outliers and extremes. Yet, surprisingly, these are what really matter.

We know this because of a strange economic principle first outlined over a hundred years ago by the Italian economist Vilfredo Pareto. Since then, it has been validated by numerous other economists and business strategists. The 'Pareto Rule' – or, as I call it, the 80/20 Principle (or simply the Principle) – is the observation that if you divide the world into causes and results, relatively few causes (roughly 20 per cent) nearly always lead to most of the results (roughly 80 per cent). Thus, a small number of people are responsible for most human progress (and indeed most human disasters). A few motorists cause the majority of accidents. A few managers determine the success or failure of their company. Time and again it has been shown that a few products, customers and decisions account for most of a firm's profits. By concentrating on the vital few customers and products – by selling more of the highly profitable products to the ultra-profitable customers – it is often possible to multiply profits many times.

Fifteen years ago, I wrote a book that extended the use of the Principle to our personal lives. In this new book, I deal with the working lives of managers, and the few things they need to do in order to maximize the results they achieve. First, I'll introduce you to the Principle and explain how it works. Fundamentally, however, this is an eminently practical book that tells you how to put the Principle into practice as easily and simply as possible. If you are allergic to numbers, you could even skip Chapter Two, which focuses on the Principle itself (although it requires no prior knowledge of, or interest in, economics and statistics). The heart of the book is Part Two, which guides you through ten ways in which to become a super-effective manager. Rest assured that all ten of those techniques are grounded in a proven economic principle, even if it seems to work in a weird and counter-intuitive way.

Half the battle of making yourself a much more effective manager lies simply in understanding the topsy-turvy world we inhabit – where most effort is a waste of time but a few well-chosen interventions can transform both your own and others' lives. As you progress through the book, you will discover many surprising insights that will revolutionize your view of life and work. For example:

- Managers need a lever if they are to make a small amount of effort go a very long way in terms of results. We will look at seven sources of leverage, some of them obvious, others less so, but all of them under-used.
- The most successful managers don't just help themselves. They help other people – in particular those who don't know each other because they move in different worlds – to connect with each other.
- Managers who are respected (and often loved) allocate a little time each week to encourage, support and guide their people. You will soon appreciate that the returns in terms of productivity and team spirit are out of all proportion to the small amount of effort required.
- Effective managers also liberate their staff, giving them the freedom to do what they do best. But it should be noted that this is not a soft option. It demands total honesty and openness on both sides, as well as the enforcement of high standards.
- Managers do not have to be short of time – in a second-pinching world they can be time-rich. The greatest results are achieved by standing back from the sound and fury that engulf almost everyone else.
- All successful careers can be crystallized to a few infrequent, but critical, decisions.
- Exceptional progress flows from combining cultivated laziness with intelligent thought and extreme ambition.

Some of the ten ways to become an exceptional manager are easy to master. Others require more effort, but only in the sense of being willing to change your approach, not the more traditional effort of hard grind and venturing down blind alleys. All ten produce a phenomenal long-term payout, not just financially but in terms of feeling good about yourself because you are making other people's lives better.

This may sound too good to be true. So is there a catch? Well, actually, there are three.

To make this new approach work for you, first you have to be willing to cast off your old assumptions and work habits. You must stop following the herd and start to think everything through for yourself. That can be tough until you get used to it.

The second catch is that you have to work in the right kind of job, for the right firm, with the right kind of boss. Broadly speaking, this means you will have the discretion to make a difference in a company that encourages rather than suppresses freedom and creativity. Unfortunately, most jobs and most companies do not fit this description. Yet, there are some of them out there, and they are quite easy to find. They tend to be highly successful, growing when most of their competitors are stagnating or declining, and they have very happy employees.

The third catch is that you must want to do something with your life. And by that I mean *really* want it, with all your heart and soul. It doesn't matter what you want to do, as long as you're serious about it.

If these three catches haven't put you off, read on. As

Karl Marx, one of the most original thinkers of the nineteenth century, said in another context, you have nothing to lose but your chains.

And you have a wonderful world to win!

PART ONE

THE QUESTION:
ARE YOU OVERWHELMED?

Chapter One: Would You Like to Simplify Your Work and Life?

Roy Grace felt increasingly that his life was a
constant challenge against the clock. As if he
was a contestant in a game show that did not
actually offer any prize for winning, because
it had no end. For every email he succeeded
in answering, another fifty came in. For
every file on his desk that he managed to
clear, another ten were brought in.

Peter James, *Dead Tomorrow*[1]

Work is overwhelming. Do you find that? Does everything
pile up in your inbox and on your desk? Do you feel like
you are always falling behind? Do you struggle to finish
your 'to-do' lists? Is it often late in the evening before you
arrive home? Do you feel constantly on call via your mobile
devices? Do you have a sinking feeling on your way to work
and a guilty feeling on the way home? Do you think that

you'll never get on top or your workload, never feel in command? Do you suspect that your bosses neither understand nor care?

If you can identify with any of those issues, I have good news for you.

Work doesn't have to be that way.

I don't deny that these pressures exist, or that they are increasing for most managers.

When I started in business, forty years ago, I worked for a large oil company. It was frustrating because there were so many layers and departments in the organization, but it was not overwhelming, and plenty of people were happy to help if I needed them. These managers were bored because their own plates were far from full. There were simple procedures to follow, clear job descriptions, and colleagues who had a great deal of time on their hands to show me the ropes.

Every Friday, the senior people in my department would head off to the pub around twelve o'clock for a two- or three-hour liquid lunch, and after a while I was allowed to tag along. During these long lunches, I learned that many of my colleagues didn't like their jobs, but I never heard any of them complain that the pressure was getting too much for them. Work was pleasantly – even unremittingly – social. There was always time to sit with your feet up, shoot the breeze, and organize your life outside of the office. Nobody – and I mean *nobody* – used to work through lunch at their desk in the 1970s.

Around this time, Robert Townsend, who developed Avis

Rent-a-Car from a tiny outfit into a highly successful international company, did something almost unique for a manager in the 1970s. He wrote a book! He was so fed up with the multiple layers of bureaucracy, the sprawling conglomerates that were increasingly remote from both workers and customers, that he unleashed a thundering volley against the fat cats who were running Corporate America, accusing them of stifling people and strangling profits. The neat title of his book was *Up the Organization*.

'In the average company,' Townsend began, 'the boys in the mailroom, the president, the vice-presidents, and the girls in the steno pool have three things in common: they are docile, they are bored, and they are dull.'[2] America had become 'a nation of office boys', 'mortals trained to serve immortal institutions'. His message to chief executives was: 'Your people aren't lazy and incompetent. They just look that way . . . Stop running down your people. It's *your* fault they're rusty from underwork.'[3]

Several of Townsend's indictments still resonate today, over forty years on. But did he really say, 'rusty from *underwork*'? That doesn't sound right to our modern ears. Perhaps he was being sarcastic. But no, he was serious. Back in 1970, there was too little managerial work to go around.

How times have changed! The excess people have long since gone. Perpetual 'restructuring' has heaped more and more work on fewer and fewer managers. The most abused word in the manager's lexicon these days is *empowerment* – a process that generously allows you to do two or three jobs instead of one. You can forget those leisurely liquid lunches. The new routine might be good for your liver, but you will be hard pressed to find enough time even to grab a sandwich around the middle of the day.

Now the watchwords are *operational excellence*, which means ever-lower costs; *commoditization*, which means making and selling goods as cheaply as possible and draining everything of personality; and *accountability*, which means that someone is routinely shafted whenever profits dip . . . and that 'someone' might well be you. If you are not prepared to play this game, rest assured that an eager beaver somewhere else in the world will gladly do it for a fraction of your salary. That is great news for customers, but it sucks for workers, managers and the company itself.

Unsurprisingly, the great majority of managers now find work overwhelming – frenzied, stressful, complex, unrelenting, exhausting and demoralizing. But a small minority have managed to buck the trend. They are optimistic, confident, relaxed and happy. They keep their work and their lives simple.

This book is about these two kinds of manager – those who are always on top of things and those who never are. If you feel you fall into the second category, the good news is that you can break out of it and join the successful 20 per cent. But before we go any further, here's a short quiz that should help you decide which type of manager you are. Give an immediate response to each question, without thinking too much.

The manager x-ray quiz

1. How long have you been in your current job?
2. How long have you been in your current organization?
3. How many hours a week do you work?
4. Do you compile 'to-do' lists?
5. Do you love your work? Do you 'tap-dance' your way to the office?
6. Is there too little time to finish everything you want to get done?
7. Have you been promoted rapidly in your career so far?
8. Do you like your boss and is he or she generally helpful?
9. Same question for your boss's boss.
10. Do you have valuable insights into your work that your colleagues do not?
11. Are you often stressed or tense at work?
12. Can you think of another job or career that you would rather have?
13. Do you talk to customers every week or nearly every week?
14. Are you pursuing a simple strategy that is working well for your unit?
15. Do you have one or more great mentors?
16. Do you regularly lunch with different acquaintances outside the firm?

Scoring

Question 1: If you've been in your current job less than two years, score 1 point. No score if you've been in it between two and four years. If you've been in it more than four years, score –2.

Question 2: If you've been in your current organization for less than four full years, you get 1 point. No score if you've been there between four and seven years. If you've been there seven years or more, score –2.

Question 3: If you work 35 hours or fewer, score 2. For 36–40 hours, score 1. No score if you work 40–49 hours. Score –2 if you work 50 hours or more.

Question 4: 2 points if you answered No. No score for Yes.

Question 5: 2 points for Yes. No points for No.

Question 6: 2 points for No. No points for Yes.

Question 7: 2 points for Yes. No points for No.

Question 8: The same.

Question 9: The same.

Question 10: The same.

Question 11: This time No gets you 2 points. Yes gets you 0 points.

Question 12: And again.

Question 13: 2 points for Yes. No points for No.

Question 14: And again.

Question 15: And again.

Question 16: And again.

Work out your total score. We'll come back to what it means at the end of the chapter.

Two ways to manage

You were probably taught the standard way to manage, or maybe you picked it up through osmosis:

- You work hard, often put in long hours, and are highly visible and available.
- You are continually busy, exhibiting a buzz of activity.
- You answer inputs from bosses and colleagues in a timely and linear way. For example, if someone sends you an email, you respond promptly. This seems perfectly natural and no more than good manners. It does, however, have the disadvantage of increasing internal communication, and the time it consumes.
- You have some discretion to think about what you are doing and do it your way, but always within the constraints of company policy, teamwork and what your bosses want.
- There is an unspoken rule that you should not be too different in style or behaviour from the bulk of your bosses and other colleagues.

In practice, this management approach quickly leads to overload. You slip behind with your work and never really catch up. Tellingly, the strain is felt most acutely in the run-up to a holiday . . . and when you return to the office.

Sometimes it can seem that work disapproves of relaxation and is determined to take its revenge.

The other way to manage is much less prevalent, but the road less travelled is more peaceful. If you are one of these rare managers:

- You generally put in fewer hours than your colleagues. You will probably work long hours occasionally, but only because you are enjoying yourself or reaching the climax of a specific project. Once it's over, you know how to relax.
- You are – unfashionably – not very action-oriented. Sometimes you might simply sit quietly at your desk, with no paper or electronic devices in sight. You spend a lot of time thinking, and a considerable amount talking, face to face. Much of your time is spent out of the office.
- You focus on outputs, not inputs. Your in-trays bulge. You have tight spam filters, but there are still a hell of a lot of unanswered emails in your inbox. Nevertheless, you often do not feel the need to respond to incoming emails or texts immediately, only answering them at particular times of the day. Each morning, you work out the one thing you want to accomplish that day. Then you do nothing else until that task is complete.
- You keep your work simple. You remove or ignore the trivial clutter that routinely strangles your colleagues. You work primarily on what can be done

quickly, yet will make a big difference. And, as far as possible, you delegate or overlook everything else.

- In a quiet way, you're a non-conformist. You are still a team player, accessible and friendly, but you often say things that surprise your colleagues. You can be inconsistent. You ask a lot of questions. You think the unthinkable. You experiment. Sometimes you take a long time to reach a decision, but once you have done so you are resolute . . . at least until you change your mind. In other words, you do things your way.

- You feel successful, although your definition of 'success' may not match anyone else's!

- Superficially, you seem quite similar to your colleagues because you don't make a big deal about your differences. Only those who know you well or work with you closely realize how unusual you are. The biggest difference of all is that you are unstressed, unhurried and usually happy.

So, is the difference between the vast majority of managers and this alternative, contented breed just a matter of temperament and personality?

No, it's not. What makes them different is not what they feel but the way they think.

They have a secret weapon . . . aside from the fact that it's not secret at all. They would be more than happy to share it with you if you asked. But almost nobody does.

Put simply, they understand the Principle. They use it every day, both inside and outside work.

But can one small piece of knowledge really explain all of their success, happiness and lack of stress?

Yes, it can. And we'll see why in the next chapter.

First, though, let's return to the quiz. Are you currently one of the overworked, overstressed majority of managers or one of the few I call '80/20 managers'. The higher your score, the more likely you are to fall into the latter category. The minimum score is –6; the maximum is 30.

If you scored 25 or more, you are already behaving like an 80/20 manager.

Between 15 and 24 means you are not yet fully an 80/20 manager, but you are on your way.

If you scored below 15 – as most managers do – that is good news, too! Yes, really. Because if you are prepared to change your approach to work you will become much happier and more effective. And why wouldn't you want to do that?

Chapter Two: The Secret Weapon

I went to a bookstore the other day. I asked
the woman behind the counter where the
self-help section was. She said, 'If I told
you that, it would defeat the whole
purpose.'

Brian Kiley

In order to do a good job of those things
that we decide to do, we must eliminate all
the unimportant opportunities.

'The Apple Marketing Philosophy', 1977[1]

At the risk of upsetting the sales assistant in Brian Kiley's
story, I am going to tell you.

The secret weapon – the thing that will turn your life
as a manager on its head and allow you to cut through
work like a chainsaw through sticky toffee – is the 80/20
Principle.

What is the 80/20 Principle?

It is the observation that a small number of events give rise to the majority of effects. Most consequences come from few causes. The great majority of outputs come from a small minority of inputs. The lion's share of results comes from a small amount of effort and energy.

We may find that 80 per cent of consequences arise from 20 per cent of causes, or that 80 per cent of outputs come from 20 per cent of inputs, or 80 per cent of results from 20 per cent of effort. Typically, 20 per cent of professional athletes will scoop 80 per cent – or more – of the competition prizes. You will wear 20 per cent – or less – of your clothes more than 80 per cent the time. A mere 20 per cent of burglars will make off with more than 80 per cent of the loot. Just 20 per cent of your car journeys will clock up more than 80 per cent of your total mileage. Only 20 per cent of your time will generate more than 80 per cent of your useful results. And 20 per cent of your decisions will lead to more than 80 per cent of your success and happiness – or the opposite.

When we collect data and test the 80/20 Principle, we usually find that most outputs flow from few inputs.

The amazing thing about the Principle is that *very few things matter at all; but those that do matter enormously*. That means most of us don't live our lives or conduct our careers sensibly, because we don't acknowledge that only very few inputs are all important. Life – especially in the workplace – conspires to make us chase numerous irrelevant objectives that sap our energy without ever giving us what we really want.

The true value of the Principle is that it helps us to identify those few activities that we should pursue because they will lead to great results.

Let's be clear. The Principle is not a theory. Nobody dreamed it up. It came from observation – from examining the relationship between a number of causes, expressed as a percentage, and a number of results, also expressed as a percentage. The observation is illuminating because we find that a few causes – approaches, methods, decisions, natural events, products, technologies, types of people, types of action, or resources of any sort – lead to results out of all proportion to the number of causes or the effort involved.

The Principle enables us to focus on the good causes, root out the bad ones, and forget about the mass of trivial and weak ones that make a lot of noise but lead to nothing except confusion. Whether we realize it or not, *all* progress – from evolution through natural selection to the latest version of the iPad – comes from conscious or unconscious experiments in which a few immensely productive events triumph at the expense of everything else. Awareness of the Principle enables us to simulate, multiply and accelerate those things we want to happen.

For example, as Walter Isaacson makes clear in his brilliant biography of Apple's founder, Steve Jobs continually focused on a handful of core products and core features – the few features that would be used most of the time – and ignored everything else.[2] In 1997, when

Jobs was reinstated as the boss of Apple, the company was near to insolvency, with only five weeks of cash flow left. But Jobs 'began slashing away at models and products. Soon he had cut 70 per cent of them. "You are bright people," he told one group. "You shouldn't be wasting your time on such crappy products."'[3] And so Apple abandoned all its non-core products, including printers, servers, and the Newton personal digital assistant, with its imperfect handwriting-recognition system. By focusing on the 30 per cent of products that generated cash, and scrapping the 70 per cent that drained it, Jobs saved the company.

Once he had identified Apple's core products, Jobs set about applying the Principle to their features. Why, for example, was the iPod such a great success? The answer is simple:

> Apple studied mp3 players and figured out the 20 percent of features that 80 percent of the users actually use, and then they figured out how to implement those features better than anyone else . . . By removing the clutter of unused features and focusing all the effort in outperforming everyone else on the features that actually matter, Apple made a world class mp3 that to this day commands an untouchably huge market share.[4]

When Apple introduced the iPhone, many commentators initially wrote it off because it lacked so many of the features boasted by the BlackBerry, such as a hardware keyboard.

But that was exactly the point. When the idea of an Apple phone was first mooted, Jobs said, 'We would sit around talking about how much we hated our phones. They were way too complicated. They had features nobody could figure out, including the address book. It was just Byzantine.'[5] The iPhone, by contrast, focused on the 20 per cent of features that everyone used more than 80 per cent of the time, made those features fun and simple to use, and presented them in a product that was thinner and lighter than any rival.

Even so, many critics predicted that the $500 iPhone would be a disaster. 'It's the most expensive phone in the world,' carped Microsoft CEO Steve Ballmer on CNBC, 'and it doesn't appeal to business customers because it doesn't have a keyboard.'[6] To some extent, Ballmer's reservations have been borne out by the sales figures: by the end of 2011, 100 million iPhones had been sold, giving Apple only a 4 per cent share of the global cellphone market. But, by selling that relatively small number of products at a relatively high price, Apple makes more than 50 per cent of the total profits enjoyed by all cellphone manufacturers (a 4/50 pattern).[7]

The Principle applies not just to products and features, but to customers, activities, the time we spend at work and outside, and even to our health and happiness. Ask yourself, for example, whose friendship you value most. Those friends are probably few in number – certainly below 20 per cent of your total number of friends – but they contribute the great majority of happiness and meaning to your life. Yet, the sad fact is that most of us spend far more time with friends, neighbours and acquaintances who are marginal to our contentment than we do with the few people who mean the most to us. Similarly, if you ask someone about the bugbears that make their life a misery, they often respond with a very short list. So isn't it a pity that so few of us act decisively to rid ourselves of these few causes of unhappiness?

Once we understand the few vital things that make us happy and most useful, the Principle enables us to reproduce, multiply and hasten the arrival of those things we want to happen. And it shows us how to cut out most of the useless white noise that has us running around in circles.

The origins of the Principle

The idea – although not the moniker '80/20' – came from an Italian economist working at Lausanne University at the end of the nineteenth century. Professor Vilfredo Pareto was studying patterns of wealth in England and realized that all the data he collected showed almost exactly the same pattern of unequal distribution. It didn't matter whether he was looking at statistics from the sixteenth century, the nineteenth century, or any other time period, a small proportion of the total population always enjoyed a very large proportion of the total wealth. Next, Pareto moved his analysis to different countries, and he was thrilled to find that Italy, Switzerland and Germany all followed an almost identical pattern. Using his accumulated data to draw graphs, Pareto devised an algebraic equation that he found applied to any wealth distribution, anywhere, at any time in history.

The graphs and equations still work today for wealth distribution, but they are equally applicable in any number of other areas, too: the incidence of earthquakes or asteroids relative to their magnitude; the ranking of cities relative to their populations; the number of weddings relative to the areas where the bride and groom lived; the number of customers and products relative to the profits they generate; and countless other relationships, both natural and man-made. In terms of results, a few very powerful causes (the most profitable customers, for example) and events (such as big earthquakes) dwarf the rest.

Pareto's work was purely descriptive. He simply observed data that researchers had painstakingly accumulated over centuries and identified a pattern. However, he could not explain that pattern. In fact, nobody has ever come up with a convincing explanation for why the Principle holds true across so many different phenomena, countries and time periods. It just seems to be the way things happen. But the more you think about it, the stranger it becomes. It contradicts our expectations.

What really fascinates me about the Principle, however, is its asymmetry, its imbalance. In most important areas of life, a *small number of events* have a *proportionately large effect*. A few people accumulate most of the wealth. A few causes have the most important results. The majority of people are silent, unheard. The minority make most of the music.

Thanks to Pareto's research, this imbalance is now entirely predictable, yet it is still nearly always unexpected. It's because the imbalance is counter-intuitive – because we don't expect it – that it's so valuable to be aware of it. Once we know how lopsided our world is, we can take advantage of it. For example, if we find that just a few customers generate most of our profits, we should focus on looking after them really well and trying to increase their purchases by providing better service and creating new products they would like. If we find that most of our customers are unprofitable, we can lower costs by cutting the service we provide to them; and we can put up their prices, secure in the knowledge that if they take their custom elsewhere, that is good for us. Such remedies go against the managerial grain, yet the Principle can give us the confidence to make such long-overdue changes.

Twitter is a fine example of the lack of balance in the world. It is a network phenomenon. When it was announced on the evening of 1 May 2011 that President Obama would make an unscheduled White House announcement, it was people using Twitter who first realized that Osama Bin Laden had been killed. At 10.24 EST, more than an hour before the broadcast, Keith Urbahn, chief of staff at Donald Rumsfeld's office, tweeted, 'So I am told by a reputable person they have killed Osama Bin Laden. Hot damn.' Within sixty seconds, Brian Stelter, a *New York Times* reporter, had retweeted this message to his followers – more than fifty thousand people. Over the next few minutes, the news became common knowledge, still a good half hour

before the official announcement. Just five people were
primarily responsible for that – Urbahn, Stelter, and three
other Twitter account holders with huge followings.[8] This
story illustrates the importance of the few in spreading
news and opinions to the many.

In March 2011, Twitter had about 175 million registered
users and the *Silicon Valley Insider* published the following
Pareto-like chart to indicate how they were using the service:

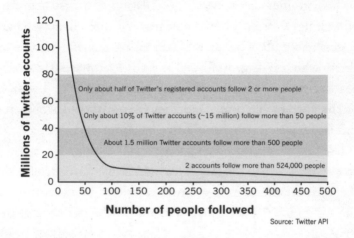

Source: Twitter API

Clearly, the number of people following other tweeters
dropped dramatically every time the 'following' threshold
was raised. Only about 9 per cent of Twitter accounts – 15
million people in 2011 – followed more than 50 tweeters,
while another 1.5 million – less than 1 per cent of users
– followed more than 500. This meant that about 10 per
cent of 'heavy followers' accounted for 85 per cent of the
total number of people followed.[9]

Consider, too, sales of the twenty books long-listed for

the UK's Orange Prize for Fiction in 2011. The total number of sales by 24 March 2011 stood at 354,000. But just one book, Emma Donoghue's *Room*, inspired by the Josef Fritzl case, accounted for 318,055 of those sales – 89.8 per cent of the total. Since one out of twenty books (5 per cent) sold 90 per cent of the total, we call this a 90/5 relationship.[10] Nevertheless, the judges awarded the prize to Téa Obreht, a twenty-five-year-old Serbian/American author, for her debut novel, *The Tiger's Wife*. At the time of writing, Obreht's book was high on the Amazon chart – at number 35 – but it was still being heavily outsold by *Room*, which was at number 13. As at October 2012, *Room* has out-sold *The Tiger's Wife* by more than 3 to 1 – sales of the former have reached 544,581, against 167,501 for the latter. [11]

I've just checked to see if there is something approaching an 80/20 pattern in the sale of my own books. Unsurprisingly, there is. Of the twenty titles I've written or co-authored, the top four – 20 per cent – account for 86 per cent of the total sales.

Another intriguing result emerged when I ranked all 263 cities in England by population, starting with London and working down, then added up the populations in the top 20 per cent of those cities – the largest 53. Those 53 cities contained 25,793,036 people, whereas all 263 had a total of 32,332,808 citizens. 25.8 million is 79.8 per cent of 32.3 million, so the top 20 per cent of cities did indeed have almost exactly 80 per cent of the people![12]

The stock market provides yet another example of

imbalance in action. At the time of writing, the latest available data was from the last quarter of 2011, when the top ten stocks on Standard & Poor's benchmark 500 Index accounted for a staggering 92 per cent of all gains, while the other 490 stocks contributed only 8 per cent. Ten out of 500 stocks – just 2 per cent – provided more than nine-tenths of the total gain: a 92/2 relationship. While it is unusual to see such extreme concentration in quarterly gains, if you take the last twenty years, more than 100 per cent of the gain in earnings from the S&P 500 has come from that same tiny proportion of the total – the top ten stocks. The index as a whole has shown robust earnings growth of 7–10 per cent per annum over the last two decades. But if you exclude the top ten stocks, the remaining 490 firms have had *negative* average growth of 3.3 per cent in the same period.

This is what I mean when I say that business is driven by extremes, not averages. Without the top ten companies, the American stock market would have sunk like a stone.

The 50/5, 20/1 and 50/1 principles

The imbalance between the *vital few* forces and the *trivial many* operates in any comparison of causes and results, even though the exact proportions will vary from one case to the next. The benchmark established so far is 80/20, but it is equally likely that the top 5 per cent of causes will account for 50 per cent of results, or that the top 1 per cent of super-potent inputs will generate 20 per cent of significant outcomes.

Let's return to Twitter. Four researchers, including the well-known network theorist Duncan J. Watts, wrote a paper in 2011 entitled 'Who Says What to Whom on Twitter'. They found that just 20,000 'elite' tweeters – less than 0.05 per cent of the total registered users – attracted almost 50 per cent of all the attention on Twitter. In round numbers that is a 50/0 relationship![13]

Can you guess what proportion of books published account for 50 per cent of total book sales? Or what proportion of companies account for half the total value of all businesses? Or what percentage of legal drugs account for half the world's pharmaceutical sales?

Most people guess that between 5 and 20 per cent of books, companies or drugs account for half the total value of their respective markets. But the correct answers, provided by Nassim N. Taleb and colleagues in the October 2009 issue of the *Harvard Business Review*, are all less than 1 per cent: 'Less than 0.25 per cent of all the companies listed in the world represent around half their market capitalization, less than 0.2 per cent of books account for approximately half their sales, and less than 0.1 per cent of drugs generate a little more than half the pharmaceutical industry's sales.'[14]

If we look at US income growth, as reported by the US Congressional Budget Office in October 2011, we find an even more extreme – and worrying – social trend. From 1983 to 2011, after correcting for inflation, US incomes rose by 62 per cent – a very large increase in historic terms. Yet most Americans do not feel much better off. The reason for this is simple: it turns out that the lowest-paid 20 per cent of American citizens enjoyed an increase of only 18 per cent over those twenty-eight years, whereas the richest 1 per cent saw their incomes soar by 275 per cent. Well over half the total increase in earnings went to the top 1 per cent.[15]

In another type of example, the historian Niall Ferguson draws attention to the remarkable intellectual influence of Jews in America:

The Jewish role in Western intellectual life in the twentieth century – especially in the United States – was indeed disproportionate . . . Accounting for around 0.2 per cent of the world's population and 2 per cent of the American population, Jews won 22 per cent of all Nobel Prizes, 20 per cent of all Field Medals for mathematics and 67 per cent of all the John Clarke Bates Medals for economists under the age of 40. Jews also won 38 per cent of the Oscars for Best Director, 20 per cent of the Pulitzer Prizes for non-fiction and 13 per cent of Grammy Lifetime Achievement Awards.[16]

There are plenty of other examples of tiny minorities exerting influence out of all proportion to their modest numbers, too:

- In 1999 two Xerox Corporation researchers found that 5 per cent of websites commanded 75 per cent of all internet traffic, 7 per cent had 80 per cent, and a mere 119 sites (far less than 1 per cent of the total), had a staggering 32 per cent of all visitors.[17]And the web has almost certainly become even more concentrated since then. Just think of the rise and rise of Yahoo and Google, both of which are millions of times more connected than your website or mine.

- Just 1.5 per cent of the world's languages are spoken by 90 per cent of people.

- A study of 300 movies released over eighteen months found that four of them – 1.3 per cent – commanded 80 per cent of total box-office receipts.[18]

- In common speech, less than 1 per cent of words are used 80 per cent of the time.

- The delightful Bill Bryson tells us that there are thirty thousand different edible plants on our planet. Yet just eleven of them account for 93 per cent of everything we eat – to the nearest whole number, that is a 93/0 relationship (as eleven is 0.04 per cent of thirty thousand). Can you name those eleven plants? I came up with potatoes, wheat, corn, rice, beans and barley.[19]

- The thriller writer David Baldacci says that 3 per cent of Washington DC's zip codes account for more than 70 per cent of the city's violent crime.[20]

What about the 'long tail'?

In 2006 Chris Anderson, in his influential book *The Long Tail*[21], proposed two new ideas:

- The internet allows relatively unpopular movies, music, books and other items to make profits – a new cultural phenomenon. For sure, he says, there will always be big hits, but the lower stockholding costs on the internet enable a 'long tail' of obscure or specialist items to be sold, catering to hitherto untapped demand. The world's largest record store can hold only 15,000 albums, but Amazon offers 250,000, while iTunes lists millions of individual tracks for download.
- Furthermore, Anderson claims that the 'long tail' will become fatter as non-hits account for a higher proportion of total sales over time. He suggests that the mass market will fragment into a plethora of niche markets, as has already happened with television. If this happens, the preponderance of hits will diminish . . . and the Principle will become less pronounced.

The great virtue of Anderson's thesis is that it can be tested. Since his book appeared, a number of studies have looked not only at the relative profitability of hits (the head of the distribution) and non-hits (the long tail), but also at how the balance between the two has changed over time.

For an article entitled 'Should You Invest in the Long Tail?', which appeared in the July–August 2008 issue of the *Harvard Business Review*, researcher Anita Elberse analysed data she obtained from Rhapsody, a website that charges a fixed monthly fee for online access to more than a million music tracks. In a three-month period in 2006, sixty thousand subscribers played thirty-two million tracks. The top 10 per cent of songs comprised 78 per cent of the total (a 78/10 pattern), while the top 1 per cent accounted for 32 per cent of all plays (32/1). Analysing data from Nielsen SoundScan on all physical and digital music sales between January 2005 and April 2007, Elberse uncovered a period of rapid change in which sales of online units soared from a third of the total to two-thirds. The tail was obviously becoming much longer, as the internet allowed customers to buy tracks by obscure artists such as the jazz saxophonist Kirk Whalum and the indie rock group the Dears. However, crucially, wrote Elberse, 'the concentration in digital-track sales is significantly stronger than in physical-album sales . . . [A]s the share of digital units grows month by month, so does the degree of concentration in sales. The tail again lengthens but flattens . . . an ever smaller set of top titles continues to account for a large chunk of the overall demand.'[22]

Elberse also looked at DVD rentals, using data from Quickflix, an Australian provider. Again, the first half of Anderson's thesis proved correct – between 2000 and 2005 the number of DVD titles that were rented only one or two times each week almost doubled.

In the same period, however, the number of titles with no sales at all in a given week quadrupled. Thus the tail represents a rapidly increasing number of titles that sell very rarely or never. Rather than bulking up, the tail is becoming much longer and flatter . . . Moreover, our research showed that success is concentrated in ever fewer best-selling titles at the head of the distribution curve. From 2000 to 2005 the number of titles in the top 10 per cent of weekly sales dropped by more than 50 per cent – an increase in concentration that is common in winner-take-all markets.[23]

So, far from overturning the Principle, as Anderson expected, analysis of the long tail demonstrates yet again that the important action still takes place at the head of the distribution. It's great that a long tail exists, but it is little more use to the modern manager than it was to the dinosaurs.

It is also telling that 80/20 trends are nearly always stronger online than offline. As the web continues to expand its market share, we should expect the benchmark to move from 80/20 to 90/10, 95/5 or even 99/1. Unsurprisingly, the executive chairman of Google, Eric Schmidt, understands this phenomenon perfectly:

I would like to tell you that the Internet has created such a level playing field that the long tail is absolutely the place to be . . . Unfortunately, that's not the case.

What really happens is something called a power law . . . a small number of things are very highly concentrated and most other things have relatively little volume. Virtually all of the new network markets follow this law. So, while the tail is very interesting, the vast majority of revenue remains in the head . . .

And, in fact, it's probable that the Internet will lead to larger blockbusters and more concentration of brands. Which, again, doesn't make sense to most people, because it's a larger distribution medium. But when you get everybody together they still like to have one superstar. It's no longer a US superstar, it's a global superstar.[24]

Why does the Principle matter to managers?

The Principle contradicts our expectations. We have the apparently reasonable idea that the many are more important than the few. The only thing is, in terms of results, that's almost never true.

In the modern world, we are tuned in to the 50/50 wavelength, not the 80/20 wavelength. We expect the world to be balanced. We expect 50 per cent of causes to lead to 50 per cent of results. We expect all events and all causes to have roughly the same significance. Whether we realize it or not, that is our universal mindset, our default assumption. But it is badly flawed.

Nowhere is this truer than in business. One of the most harmful, ridiculous, idiotic, yet enduring assumptions of the business world is that *all* sales are good, *all* revenue is valuable, and *all* sources of revenue are of roughly equal importance. They are not.

The delusion that all revenue is good drives the worst and most palpably absurd blunders in the business world. It leads to enormous amounts of energy and money being wasted in chasing totally unsuitable customers, typically the smaller and less sophisticated ones: nine times out of ten, any new customers that are acquired will do nothing to increase profits. It also drives expensive and sometimes fatal acquisitions. Think of AOL's purchase of Time Warner in 2000 for $164 billion. Bob Pitman, AOL's president, justified the cost by saying, 'All you need to do is put a catalyst [to Time Warner] and, in a short period, the growth rate will be like an Internet company.' If he was talking about the growth of losses, he was absolutely right. Two years later, AOL/Time Warner made a loss of $99 billion, and AOL's total value fell from $226 billion to less than a tenth of that.

The same misguided assumption encourages expansion into new products that have limited appeal among the firm's core customers, or don't fit its channels of distribution and brand positioning. Think of Coca-Cola's disastrous attempts to sell fruit juices and health drinks. It also drives forays into foreign markets where conditions and rivals are different, and where local competitors enjoy numerous hidden advantages. Think of respected UK retailer Marks & Spencer's rash move into the American market, including the expensive acquisition of Brooks Brothers and Kings

Super Markets, as well as its failures in Canada, France and, of all places, Afghanistan.

The assumption that all sales are good leads to profitless growth. Unwary managers attach roughly the same importance to new, disaffected and/or complaining customers – who buy little, demand unfeasibly low prices, and demoralize staff and other customers – as they do to loyal, long-standing and enthusiastic customers who pay the full whack, recommend products to friends, and improve the morale of the company's best employees.

So why do otherwise good managers make these mistakes?

Because they think the world is 50/50. They think that results flow from causes in a linear and roughly equal way. They think that all revenues lead to profits. They think in *averages*.

They don't understand that the world is really 80/20. One customer is *not* as good as another. One business segment or product is *not* as good as another. One dollar of sales is *not* worth as much as the next dollar.

It is likely that only about one-fifth of customers are worth around four-fifths of a company's value; which means that the other four-fifths are worth only one-fifth. If you do the sums, you realize that one core customer is worth *sixteen times* one ordinary customer. That's an amazing figure, so it's no wonder that we find it hard to believe. And it's no surprise that we neglect to act on it. But it's true. And the 'sixteen times' figure crops up in numerous other aspects of the 80/20 world, too.

Say, for instance, that one hundred of your employees

are making one hundred units of a certain product. Well, according to our benchmark, just twenty of them will probably be responsible for eighty of those units. On average, then, each of these super-performers is creating four units. Meanwhile, the other eighty employees are creating just twenty units between them. On average, each of these under-performers is creating just a quarter of a unit.

So it takes sixteen of the under-performing people ($16 \times 0.25 = 4$) to create the same number of products as one super-performer is producing on their own. The super-performers are sixteen times more productive than the under-performers. This is the breakthrough principle of sixteen times.

For an activity to go from the normal 'under-performing' level to the 'super-performing' level, it must improve by sixteen times. Of course, that's only precisely true if the imbalance is precisely 80/20, which is unlikely. But an improvement of between ten and twenty times, or better, is nearly always feasible.

In fact, my own research indicates that 80/20 might *understate* the degree of imbalance. In one recent case, data show that 116 per cent of a firm's profits can come from just 18 per cent of its customers. The rest, as a group, are often loss making. Other studies, carried out on behalf of leading North American banks, have found similar results. One, for the Royal Bank of Canada, based in Toronto, showed that 17 per cent of customers accounted for 93 per cent of the company's profits. The others concluded that between 15 and 25 per cent of customers yielded 80 to 95 per cent of profits.[25]

Only 12 per cent of American households use personal financial management software. Yet those few households generate 75 per cent of the profits made by all US banks.

The value of 80/20 thinking is that it can change your mindset from a widely accepted yet wholly inaccurate way of viewing the world to one that is harder to believe, but infinitely more accurate. 50/50 thinking is the modern equivalent of the maps that Columbus and other explorers used in the fifteenth century. 80/20 thinking is like Google Earth. It shows the true picture with devastating clarity, warts and all. The Principle provides a new window on the world – one that is hard to accept and understand but gives us rare insight and radically improves our effectiveness.

Can you imagine what work would be like if you always made 80/20 decisions?

You would never be short of time. You would deal only with the most important and intriguing issues. You would make your business much more effective and profitable. You would be able to tell your colleagues how to make their jobs easier and more fun. You would identify your best customers and know how to make them happier than ever. You would appreciate the business's true strengths, those rare and valuable things that give it an advantage over all its competitors.

Envisage the sense of calm and quiet self-assurance you would enjoy if you could routinely get to the heart of any issue and pinpoint the few crucial elements that really matter . . . and have the confidence not to waste time on the many arduous tasks that are unimportant.

The Principle is your passport to this work paradise. Part Two explains how it is put into practice.

PART TWO

THE ANSWER: TEN WAYS TO BE AN 80/20 MANAGER

Now comes the practical bit.

Don't be daunted by the fact that there are ten different ways. Think of them as a menu from which you can pick and choose, not a checklist of skills that you must master. Getting on top of just one of the ten ways – which is not hard at all – could make all the difference for you. A one-course meal may be more than enough.

The profound truth about the 80/20 Principle is that there are multiple routes to results and success. You don't need balance. In fact, being brilliant at one of the ten ways will take you an awful lot further than being competent at all ten.

So feel free to dip into the book as you see fit. I would advise selecting the one way that appeals to you most, then working on it. You'll see results very quickly, but each way is also quite profound, so you might still be learning how to master it six months, a year, or even a decade from now.

Each of the ways offers a great payback on the effort you put in. So you might decide to become proficient in one . . . then another . . . and maybe then another. You might decide to perfect two or three ways. Or you might aim to acquire the entire portfolio of skills over a number of years.

Another option is to be eclectic – mix and match the particular techniques that appeal the most from several different ways and construct your own unique blend of low-effort, high-result managerial skills.

It's entirely up to you.

I should say frankly that some of the ways are easier than others. I've put the easy ones at the beginning, and the harder ones at the end. But, of course, you may find you have a natural affinity for one of the 'harder' ways, in which case go for it.

Remember, this is not a test. You have plenty of time. Take it slowly, and don't be surprised if you are still learning how to master some of these techniques in ten years' time. But if you want work to be easier and more fun, and want to achieve hugely better results, you need to put these ideas into practice and start making much better decisions right away.

Don't just read this book. Think of it as a quarry of behaviour-changing nuggets that you can deploy to make you the best possible manager you can be.

Way One: The Investigating Manager

> Curiosity is more important than knowledge.
>
> Albert Einstein

The business of organizing

What do you do when you know you have a problem but don't know how to fix it? That was the question some associates and I had to grapple with in 1990, when we took a controlling stake in Filofax. The iconic personal organizer company had seen its sales slump after a surge in the mid-1980s. When we got our hands on it, Filofax was losing money fast. In another few months, it would be bust.

The first thing we did was investigate what was wrong. With the Principle in the back of our minds, we wanted to know if there were a few core products that still made a good return, and if others were heavily loss-making.

The company made two main products – the leather six-ring binder; and the pre-printed sheets, including a calendar/diary, that went inside it – but we needed to know which binders and inserts might be viable and which were a dead loss. A quick walk round the warehouse was illuminating. The shelves were stuffed with a most extraordinary inventory. The binders came in all shapes and sizes, and numerous coverings. A lot of them were apparently made from the hide of karungs. We had no idea what a karung was, but the piles of unsold stock suggested that they had died in vain. Then we came across the mounds of paper inserts. These were neatly stacked by subject, and there were an awful lot of subjects. In the first few minutes, we found inserts for bird-watching, bridge, chess, photography, windsurfing . . . you name it. There were tens of thousands of each, and they looked like they had been there a very long time.

That tour of the warehouse gave us our first 80/20 hypothesis. There were three or four main binders and inserts. The most popular was a 'standard fill' that included the year's calendar, space to write in meetings, and some popular pages such as the New York Subway and London Underground maps. We guessed – or at least hoped – that the half dozen or so favourite products might make some money. But the great majority had to be a liability.

And so it proved when we investigated further. Just 4 per cent of stock-keeping units (SKUs) generated 93 per cent of Filofax's revenue. These top products made a generous 20 per cent profit on sales. The other 96 per cent were hugely unprofitable.

Then we found that 20 per cent of our customers – the retailers who sold the organizers – accounted for 91 per cent of our total sales. Our next step was to ask those retailers what the problem was. They said the organizers were too expensive. A new rival, Microfile, was offering something similar for half our price and had captured a lot of Filofax's sales. Suddenly we realized that the old management had been mistaken. They had presumed that the whole market had collapsed. But it hadn't; only our *market share* had.

We asked our retailers if we had to price our products as low as Microfile. They said no – Filofax could still command a price premium, but it should be 10–15 per cent, not 50 per cent. We cut our prices accordingly, and made sure our costs were as low as Microfile's. Cutting costs was easy because we streamlined our product range and our organizers started to sell well again at the new, lower price level. Within three years, volumes had quadrupled and we were making good profits. When we sold the company, our investors made seven times their money.

A questioning mind

Children learn to ask questions very early on, opening new windows on their world. Questions enable them to piece together connections in the mystery of life and understand how they fit into the big picture. The speed of their personal development depends on the number and quality of the questions they ask, and their determination to make sense of existence. If you have toddlers, you will see this wonderful, strange, staggering, miraculous, impressive and effective process every day.

As we grow older, though, we tend to stop asking questions and start offering answers – usually not especially original ones. We stop thinking. Our awe for life's enigmas disappears. Having gained *some* mastery of our environment, we accept it as a given. Because we stop asking questions, we lose the ability to uncover fresh patterns. Life becomes less mysterious, more dull.

Detectives are different, which is why murder mysteries fascinate so many people. Fictional investigators – from Sherlock Holmes to Inspector Rebus – are impelled to find the answer to a particular question: *whodunnit?* They achieve this by thinking the unthinkable and investigating seemingly unpromising leads. The answer, when it finally comes, has to be original and unexpected. Detectives – and some scientists – are among the few adults who still think like children. They get their kicks by asking questions and increasing their knowledge as a result.

Managers should behave in the same way. Asking questions and not automatically believing what everyone else believes, or accepting everything you are told – in other words, investigative thinking – is an 80/20 activity. It yields occasional insights that turn reality on its head and enable you to move to a higher plane of existence. Investigation reveals an unsuspected, subterranean world – an intriguing realm where what we think is good might be bad, where there are all kinds of hidden links, where an apparently trivial event can trigger an avalanche, where strong emotions lurk, powerfully disrupting the surface calm.

In business, the most potent type of investigation looks beyond averages, because averages can be misleading. Business is not driven by averages; it is driven by exceptions, extremes. Beneath the average there are always a few good forces and a mass of mediocre or bad ones. The investigating manager's mission is to work out which is which. Once you get in the groove, investigation gives you an edge as well as a level of excitement that most managers do not even know exists.

Investigation is fun. If you ask the right questions, it is also relatively easy. Using the 80/20 methodology, you will learn to ask a few crucial questions that will provide all the answers you need.

The most pertinent question of all is:

Are a few products or customers super-profitable?

Here's a clue: the answer is always yes!

Now all you have to do is identify those super-profitable products and customers.

And, for an encore, work out which are the really disastrous ones . . .

Who are your core customers and what makes them different from the rest?

The 80/20 benchmark suggests that roughly four-fifths of your profits will come from just one-fifth of your customers. These are the *core customers* with whom you have a mutually beneficial love affair and they are absolutely crucial for your firm's future. Yet many managers do not even know who their core customers are, let alone understand why they are so important. A typical mistake is to think that *most* customers are important. This is nearly always a delusion: only your core customers really matter. Once you appreciate that, identify who they are and focus on them, you will find that your profits increase with relatively little effort.

So why do most managers remain in the dark, concentrating on the many unimportant clients and neglecting the crucial few? The answer is that accounting systems are built on averages, not extremes. Your job is to build a new system by investigating your customer base, identifying a pattern that is 80/20 (or even more lopsided) and then focusing on the 20 per cent.

I recently studied an online trading business and found that just 17 per cent of the firm's customers provided 122 per cent of its profits. The other 83 per cent were loss-making. At first sight, it seemed very easy to categorize the company's clients into good or bad for business: *amateur* traders – enthusiasts who had some money and enjoyed trading, but didn't do it for a living – were much more profitable than the *professionals*. But looking at the amateur traders as a group didn't tell the full story. Although, as a group, the amateurs were nicely profitable, that average hid what *really* mattered.

When I peeled the onion further, I found that size mattered (as it so often does). The small amateur traders were extremely *unprofitable*; and even the medium-sized ones were loss-makers, although to a lesser extent. The explanation for this was simple. The cost of recruiting the traders (known as the 'acquisition cost' among sales and marketing folk) outweighed any profit the business accrued from their trades. This was because they didn't do much trading when they visited the website *and* they tended not to stick around for too long.

By contrast, a handful of really big amateur traders were enormously profitable for the business. It cost the company almost nothing to recruit them as they were enthusiasts who would have crawled over broken glass to reach the firm's website anyway. They liked the product so much that they recommended it to fellow fanatics. And they were so happy with the service – which was much more user-friendly and fun than anything provided elsewhere – that they gladly paid more commission than the professionals. Moreover, these sophisticated amateurs were a great help in developing and road-testing new products. A stream of such products enabled the firm to increase its revenues with each enthusiastic customer over time. They were the polar opposite of the small, unsophisticated amateurs who often got bored with the service and left before the company could make any return on its investment of recruiting them.

Once we had identified the high-value customers, we

nurtured them like crazy. First we redesigned the website to suit their needs. Then we developed new products at their behest, including mobile and iPad applications that they particularly demanded. Finally, we started to pay them handsomely for recommending the company to friends with similar profiles. Meanwhile, we put far less effort (and money) into recruiting smaller customers, and raised existing small customers' commission rates.

Naturally, revenues started to grow and profits surged.

Your business will almost certainly have a similarly small number of profitable clients. They will tend to be:

- Your most loyal and long-standing customers.
- Those who are most appreciative of the firm and the products or services you provide.
- Those who are most aligned with your offerings. For instance, if your products are pioneering, advanced or upscale – such as those of Rolex or Bang & Olufsen – your best customers will be similarly sophisticated. On the other hand, if your products are marked as value for money – such as those of Timex or Bush – your best customers will be happy with that standard.
- Those who are the least price sensitive.
- Those who complain the least.
- Your biggest customers. Although beware of big customers who have none of the attributes above because they may use their muscle to demand ruinous prices.

It can be equally valuable to identify your biggest *problem customers*, the real loss-makers whom you can afford to lose. You should be bold in raising your prices for these people, and/or cutting the costs of serving them. The worst customers are mirror-images of the best. They tend to be:

- The most promiscuous – they shop around and will drop you in a heartbeat when a rival offers a special promotion.
- The most price sensitive – which is a cheek, since they are invariably very expensive to serve.
- Compulsive complainers.
- Badly aligned with your product or service because they really want something either more sophisticated or more basic.
- The most expensive customers to acquire.

Once you have identified these extremely good and bad customer groups, you need to work out the full price realization of each group, and the full costs of serving them, including an accurate calculation of all overheads, such as sales and marketing, administration and research. Beware of using average data. For example, if one customer group is more price sensitive than another, the 'cheapo' group will buy more when your goods are on special offer, so the price you get from them will be lower, but this won't show up in any existing accounting data. You may need to take a sample of each customer group and observe or estimate the effect of their different behaviour. Similarly, the full cost of attracting a new customer in each group must be set against how long they are likely to remain loyal to the company and how much they will spend during that time. Acquiring small and temporary customers is often incredibly uneconomic, but you won't see that until the sums are done.

Working out customer profitability is a serious and difficult task, so don't attempt to do it yourself unless you are a trained accountant. Give the job to your finance department or even call in outside consultants. Your job is simply to tell them which customer groups to test.

Which are your most profitable product lines . . . and which are the turkeys?

As with working out who your most valuable customers are, the trick for products lies in coming up with ideas to test. You should divide your products into groups that you think *might* exhibit extremely good or bad profitability. The best product lines are likely to be the few that:

- Sell in *much* higher volumes than the rest.
- Were developed and introduced a long time ago.
- 'Run themselves' without anybody having to think about them.
- Are not made by rival firms (or are sold in much lower volumes by those firms).
- Have high and stable prices.

- Utilize the firm's 'power alleys' – its superior and distinctive technologies, supply chains, proprietary ideas or processes and highly qualified staff.

The much larger number of big cash drains are probably:

- Selling slowly.
- 'Specials' that require a lot of thought, selling, or adjustment to meet bespoke client demands (and never command enough of a price premium to justify all the effort).
- New or recently introduced products, especially if they require expensive advertising, marketing or selling.
- Items that competitors can produce and sell just as well, particularly if they have higher volumes.
- Products whose prices fluctuate, and tend to fall over time.
- Products with a high proportion of 'bought-in' costs, especially if the key component suppliers are in a strong bargaining position. For example, most car-makers buy in not only the metal and other components but the electronics, so a high proportion of the total manufacturing cost is bought in.
- Products that don't need the high skill level that others require.

Once you have used these lists to divide your products into 'good' and 'bad', you will be in a position to ask what is perhaps the most important question of all.

What is your firm's 'core'?

Just as a few products and a few customers really count, while most of the rest drag down your profits, so most of a firm's *activities* are largely irrelevant, while a few are extraordinarily important and give the business its reason to exist.

This is the concept of the 'core'. It consists of the 1–20 per cent of what your company does (and what it *is*) that makes you different from any other firm in your sector and delivers most of your value to the world.

Firms without a strong core don't become well known. Nor do they last long.

Firms with a strong core can change the world.

Two professors at Harvard Business School, David Collis and Cynthia Montgomery, talk about a business's 'core resources' – its small number of central capabilities.[1] You may have heard the expression 'core competencies', but I think the idea of 'core resources' is richer and more useful, as it encompasses not just what the firm does well but its physical assets, such as a great location, and its intangible assets, such as a great brand or the ability to work in a unique way.

Collis and Montgomery provide five criteria that will help you identify the resources that are truly core in your business. To qualify as core, a resource must pass all five of these criteria, so you will not find many of them. It must be:

- Hard to copy. For example, you might be in a great location that is not available to rivals.
- Depreciate (lose value) slowly. For example, the Disney brand was neglected for more than twenty years before Michael Eisner took over as boss in 1984. Yet the brand, embodied in such icons as Mickey Mouse and Donald Duck, retained its latent value and could be revived to great effect.
- Controlled by the company, not by employees, suppliers or customers. A while back I advised Libra, a consortium bank owned by world-leading banks. Libra had particular expertise in investment banking in Latin America, which you might think was a core resource, but it wasn't, because a close-knit team of about thirty investment bankers made all the profits for the business. I pointed out this vulnerability to the head of the bank, but he couldn't do anything about it. Sure enough, a couple of years later, the profit-making team was headhunted by Morgan Grenfell. Libra never recovered from the blow.
- Secure against substitution by a new product, service or technology. I mentioned Filofax earlier. Its core resource was the clever design of its personal organizer, which contained all of the user's vital social and business data. In the 1990s, however, electronic organizers started to appear. Although they were initially clunky and slow, and so scarcely dented Filofax's sales for a few years, we knew that they would eventually come to dominate the

personal organizer market. We were lucky enough to sell Filofax before this happened, before it became apparent to everyone else that our core resource was no longer core.

- Clearly superior to any rival's comparable resource. For example, Coca-Cola's core resource is not its product formulation but its brand, which is deeply embedded in the American psyche and around the world, usually by virtue simply of being the *first* cola to appear on the market. Blind tests consistently show that a majority of people prefer Pepsi to Coke, yet Coke outsells Pepsi in most markets because its core resource, its brand, is all-conquering.

If you are ruthless in testing your own firm's resources against these criteria, you will typically find that it has only one or two core resources. Once you establish what they are, you can focus everyone's energy on building them up. As a result, your company will soon have a much greater impact on the world.

Seven questions you should ask yourself

A successful investigative manager needs to turn their microscope on more than just the firm and its products. A series of more personal '80/20 questions' will help you get the best out of yourself, too.

Which single powerful idea will turbo-charge my business . . . and my career?

There is an almost infinite number of ideas in the world. However, investigate only those that have been successful elsewhere – in another country or another firm, for example – and you will greatly improve your own chances of success. Then, having explored all the options, choose just *one* that has the best chance of making an enormous impact.

The experience of a good friend of mine, Jamie Reeve, perfectly illustrates just how successful this technique can be. He was thirty-two and a junior manager at the BBC when he started to ponder what he was doing with his life:

By the summer of 1996, I'd been at the BBC for eighteen months. I worked in the Strategy Department and I was bored stiff. I didn't find strategy for television and radio terribly interesting – it was an endless debate about tactical scheduling to gain tiny movements in audience share.

I decided to take a break and hopped on a plane to visit my friend Mark Davies in New York. He'd worked in publishing and had created a listings magazine, like *Time Out*. But he'd recently discovered he could make the information available via the nascent internet. He was excited that people would come and visit his database over the web. He wasn't trying to make money. He just liked being able to marshal information and share it with many other people. He never earned a cent of revenue. (Actually, he sold the business a year later for eight million dollars, but that's a different story!)

Soho was full of similar businesses run by smart but laid-back dudes. Change was in the air. I was wearing a suit to work and sat at a formal desk in a dull office. Mark didn't own a suit. He worked off a trestle table made from an old door, and shared a tatty but cool loft with three other small businesses. I felt like an eighteenth-century peasant seeing my first cotton mill. As Bob Dylan might have said, something was going on, even if I didn't know what it was.

I came back full of beans, wondering how the internet would change London, and how I could take part in that. I reckoned I needed to jump ship from the BBC. But then something uncanny happened, as I think it often does when you have an obsession . . .

Who might sponsor the idea?

Once you have identified your single great idea, don't be afraid to shout about it. Someone high up in your organization, maybe at the very top, might be interested in what you have to say, as Jamie discovered:

It turned out that my boss, who reported to John Birt [the Director-General at the time], had been told by him to find out more about the internet. Although she was an excellent manager, she and the rest of her team were suspicious of the 'new new thing' – she was a charming technophobe! She asked for a volunteer to take on the internet project and I was delighted to be the only one to step forward.

I plucked up my courage and went to see John Birt. He was not popular with the broadcasters, but he had a reputation for being open to new ideas and I heard he was trying to break the stranglehold of the old guard by surrounding himself with young people. I knew that he liked America and kept in touch with trends there. He had produced David Frost's landmark interviews with Richard Nixon, which obliged the former President to admit, for the first time, that he had let the American people down over Watergate.

Birt had just come back from another trip to the West Coast and was intrigued by the internet, but unclear about its implications. Like me, he sensed it was a game-changer. We were both surprised by the other's enthusiasm. 'Let's go together to Silicon Valley for a week in July,' he said. 'I don't mind who we see as long as they are internet pioneers. And we must finish at 4 p.m. on the Friday as I need to be back in Seattle then.'

Microsoft, of course, is based in Seattle, so John was hinting we should visit their campus at Redmond. How was I supposed to organize that? I called the Microsoft rep managing the BBC account and asked if he could arrange a tour for us. I didn't hold my breath. But half an hour later he called back to say it was all fixed, and we could meet 'Bill'.

That was how John and I came to listen – mesmerized – for over an hour to Bill Gates as he rapped about the difference the internet was going to make. I became head of digital strategy for the BBC, and four months later we launched BBC Online. It now has more than ten million users and is the most popular non-American content site in cyberspace.

Who is achieving great results and how?

If you see someone achieving great success, there is always a reason why. If you discover it, you might be able to emulate and/or adapt their methods and achieve similar results yourself.

Here I think we can learn a great deal from two of my former employers – the consulting firms Boston Consulting Group (hereafter BCG) and Bain & Company (Bain). Bill Bain worked for BCG until leaving to launch the firm that bears his name. In those years BCG was organized into four colour-coded teams (red, yellow, blue and green). Each of these had the same number of consultants, but they were anything but equal in terms of results. Bain's team far outperformed the other three because he was already putting into practice his aim to gain huge budgets within individual clients. He understood the Principle and implemented it as best he could at BCG, but he knew that the way forward was to have far fewer clients and to develop far deeper relationships with them. This involved the complete transformation of the client through the consulting intervention, which was precisely the approach that Bill adopted once he launched his own firm. For Bill Bain, less was more.

How do I achieve a sixteenfold improvement?

As we saw in Chapter Two, there is usually room for vast improvement in performance. And understanding the Principle will give you the confidence to achieve it. Don't be satisfied with something that is just two or three times better – aim for sixteen times or more. Pursue seemingly outrageous progress. Visualize what this would be like. For example, picture a bicycle in a race against a Ferrari. No matter how much work you put into improving the bicycle, it will never get close to the Ferrari.

So you need to learn how to drive the sports car. You need a totally different approach to achieve your goal.

How can I achieve much more with much less?

Ernest Rutherford (1871–1937) was the New-Zealand-born scientist who split the atom. From 1919, he ran the path-breaking Cavendish Laboratory at Cambridge University. A team of American scientists once visited him there, but they were not impressed, expressing consternation at the small and poorly equipped lab.

'It's true we don't have much money,' Rutherford replied, 'so what we have to do is think.'

His motto was: 'Seek the first principles'. A little thought about first principles can save you millions. And lacking infinite time and money prompts invention. Whenever we think about achieving a great deal more, our first inclination

– especially if we work within a large and well-funded enterprise – is to think we need *more* people, *more* money, *more* time. It is salutary to take the opposite approach. It leads to breakthroughs, big or small.

When I helped run a consulting firm in the 1980s, one of the banes of my life was voicemail (this was before email). I would come into work in the morning and find interminable messages, mostly from overseas. It took me a good hour or two of prime time to wade through them and answer them. I resented this daily chore, so my answers were often cursory and unhelpful, bordering on the bad-tempered.

Eventually I asked myself how I might cut the time I spent on voicemail by 90 per cent and do a better job on it. To ask the question was to answer it. I delegated the task of listening to the messages to my secretary, asked her to deal with 90 per cent of them and got her to summarize the remaining 10 per cent for me in no more than five minutes. Finally, I dictated a reply: 'Richard thanks you for your voicemail,' she would tell those who demanded a response, 'and asked me to say . . .' whatever. Soon she was dealing with 95–100 per cent of the calls without any involvement from me. And she was much more diplomatic and effective than I had ever been!

The moral of this story is that you can always achieve better results through less effort. All it takes is a bit of thought and imagination.

Who is my most important customer?

I failed to ask this critical question when I worked for BCG in the latter half of 1970s. I assumed the way to get ahead was to build relationships with my clients. While I had some success at this, I neglected the other vital step of pleasing my immediate bosses – the project manager and the company vice-president, in this case. *They* were my most important customers. At the time, I didn't realize the importance of patronage, of cultivating the support of a powerful boss, of doing what they wanted and working out what else would please them. The VP said I made him nervous at client meetings, because he never knew what I was going to say. (I had a tendency to go off-message when responding to a client when I should have just shut up.) He also said I exploded like a volcano from time to time. Too true.

When I joined Bain & Company in 1980, at the age of thirty, I suppressed my flamboyant side and single-mindedly put into practice what my core customer (my boss) wanted. That was the main difference between a failing career and a thriving one. Four-fifths of how you are viewed by the powers that be may rest on the opinions of just one or two highly influential people in your organization. It's a bit like the Mafia, except that at work you may be able to choose your godfather or godmother.

A new and powerful core customer can spark off a nuclear reaction *in* you and *for* you. For instance, Jamie Reeve's career at the BBC took off when John Birt became his core customer. There was little or no point in expending valuable time and energy cultivating good relationships with all of the others. By focusing on his project with the Director-General, Jamie was able to leap over more than a hundred people in the BBC hierarchy and get to do something that really turned him on – build BBC Online.

Your most important customer is the person to whom you can add the greatest value and with whose help you can transform the scale and impact of what you do. That person may be your direct boss, another of the higher-ups, someone who is clearly going places in the organization, an actual customer or client, or someone with whom you collaborate outside the firm. The crucial point is that you need to identify them and then learn how to impress them.

Which single constraint is holding me back?

In 1941, the electrical engineer Joseph Moses Juran came across the Principle. It helped him develop his theories of quality control, which subsequently became immensely influential in Japan after the war. Juran trained top and middle managers to manage for quality, until Japanese industrial standards eventually outstripped those of the United States. In the 1980s, in a bid to catch up, US businesses belatedly started to adopt the same techniques. Juran used what he called the 'Rule of the Vital Few' (the Principle, in other words) to concentrate on the small number of – or sometimes single – cause of quality failure that accounted for most defects.

There may be many reasons for success, but there are usually only one or two principal reasons for personal failure.

For some managers, it's a lack of confidence or knowledge. For others, it's fear – of the overwhelming workload, the boss, the organization, peers or even subordinates. For some, it's as simple as a lack of engagement, excitement and interest. It is hard to shine when you are bored.

So what is holding *you* back? Be honest. Without facing this issue head on, you may end up wasting your entire working life. The most important investigation you can make is into your own psyche. Identify your core abilities and, especially, your core problem. If you know what is holding you back, you can do something about it. Remove the constraint and power ahead!

Ask your way to success

The great thing about the key questions contained in this chapter is that anyone can ask them. Yet, in a few short weeks, they should unlock the secrets of exceptional success (and failure) that have eluded your colleagues for years. You will know which 20 per cent of your customers to nurture, which 20 per cent of your products to promote, which core customer to cultivate. After that, the hard work (or at least 80 per cent of it) will be over.

I hope you agree that there is nothing particularly difficult about asking these questions or indeed, in most cases, working out the answers. As you run through them, you will probably find that other lines of enquiry pop up into your mind, and before long you will have rediscovered much of the marvellous curiosity you had when you were very young. In turn, that will enable you to make fresh discoveries about the riddles inherent in all but the simplest businesses. Once you have solved the riddles, successful management is child's play.

As long as you keep investigating – and you won't be able to stop yourself – you will have mastered one of the ten ways to become a fully fledged 80/20 manager.

The next chapter reveals another undemanding yet rewarding way to become an 80/20 manager. Sociological and psychological research has revealed the importance of gathering fresh ideas from the people in the background of our lives, especially those who move in different circles to our own. It turns out that the best connections in business and life are often the least expected . . . and usually the most neglected.

Way Two: The Superconnecting Manager

It is remarkable that people receive crucial
information from individuals whose very
existence they have forgotten.

Professor Mark Granovetter[1]

Creativity comes from spontaneous meetings,
from random discussions. You run into someone,
you ask what they're doing, you say 'Wow', and
soon you're cooking up all sorts of ideas.

Steve Jobs[2]

Weak links, powerful effects

Who do you think can provide the most help in your work
and life? Your close colleagues? Friends and family? Or
people you hardly know and rarely see?

The answer is surprising. Great leaps forward in our lives – such as getting a fantastic new job or finding the key to transforming a business – are more likely to come out of blue, from casual acquaintances, than from our close friends and colleagues. The art of being a *superconnecting* manager is cultivating a wide range of diverse casual acquaintances, and fully utilizing the 'weak links' we all have in profusion. I shall use an important turning-point in my own life as an illustration.

When I was thirty-three and working for Bain & Company, two colleagues and I decided to start our own consulting firm, LEK. It was hard. Bain & Company sued us and stopped us taking our clients with us, something we had banked on being able to do. Our small pot of capital was dwindling fast and we desperately needed to find a big client. We called all our friends and close business contacts, but that didn't get us anywhere. Finally, the three of us sat down to work out what to do next. Iain and I were glum; Jim was more upbeat and can-do. Iain and I put it down to him being American.

'Here's what we should do,' Jim said. 'Take a sheet of paper and write down the name of *every* manager you know who works in a large company. Include everyone, even if you don't know them that well – former colleagues, acquaintances from college or business school, friends of friends. Don't worry if you haven't seen them for years. Take them out to lunch or for a drink after work to catch up. Tell them what you are doing and see if they have any ideas.'

That was how I ended up in Julie's Wine Bar near the

Portobello Road in London with Nicholas Walt, a distinguished-looking former colleague from BCG. He was tall and slender; his signature trait was walking with a ramrod-straight back, like an old soldier. We had vaguely known each other five years earlier, had never worked or socialized together, but had got on well in the office and shared a subversive sense of humour. I'd met him twice since leaving BCG, when he had tried to hire me for a large firm.

The wine acted as an effective anaesthetic as he rattled off a long series of stories about the delights of becoming a father in his early fifties. I tried to steer the conversation to his role within the Imperial Group, one of Britain's largest conglomerates, with interests in tobacco, food manufacturing, leisure, restaurants and hotels, but all Nick wanted to talk about was how his son had given him a new lease of life. If his boy was gurgling with pleasure, so was his dad.

Eventually, though, I managed to stem the flow and explained that we were finding it very tough to get our new venture up and running. The phone simply didn't ring as it had when I was in a big firm.

Nick empathized: 'The strain must be enormous,' he said. But all I got out of him that evening was another glass of wine and some sympathy.

So it was something of a surprise when I answered the phone two weeks later and heard Nick on the other end of the line. He started asking questions about the size of our firm. I admitted there were only seven of us.

'Hmm,' he said.

There was an extremely long pause.

I said nothing.

'Well,' he eventually resumed, 'I wanted to tell you that our food division is organizing a beauty parade of strategy consultants. We've made a short list of McKinsey and BCG. I'll see if I can get you invited to make a presentation, too. Individually you have a lot of high-level experience, even if your new firm is tiny. Don't expect them to pick you for such a big assignment, but pitching will be good experience for you.'

To cut a long story short, McKinsey was selected while we were congratulated on coming second. We were quite pleased with that – it was good to be mentioned in such illustrious company. (McKinsey and BCG were the world's biggest and most acclaimed strategy consultancies at the time.) But then, at the very last minute, after a restless night, Gerry Sharman, the boss of the food division, had a change of heart. Gerry was a tough old bird who had come up the hard way, and he didn't like McKinsey's 'snootiness'. He also thought we had made the best presentation. So, in the end, he offered us the contract. The other two firms were taken aback, which pleased Gerry immensely.

Later we worked with other Imperial divisions, and ultimately at the corporate level. But that first contract came at a critical time for our firm. It gave us the confidence to hire aggressively and helped us win other major clients. Without it, who knows what might have become of our fledgling firm?

At the time, I viewed it as a stroke of pure luck, given that it had arisen from a contact so weak that I had almost not even bothered to call Nick and suggest a quick drink after work. I met up with him a couple of times over the next few years and of course thanked him profusely, but as I write this I'm ashamed to say that we haven't spoken for twenty-one years. Not even a call or an email. Nevertheless, that chat in Julie's Wine Bar was a critical moment in my life. When I left LEK six years later, I had enough money to do whatever I wanted thereafter. Largely thanks to Nick Walt.

Weak links – information provided by acquaintances – are often more powerful than the supposedly strong links of close friends and family. Long after my encounter with Nick, I discovered that a sociologist called Mark Granovetter had written a seminal paper about 'The Strength of Weak Ties'.[3] His Ph.D. project at Harvard had focused on how managers got new jobs. To his surprise, his research revealed that most managers found their jobs – especially prestigious and well-paid jobs – through personal contacts rather than through advertisements, formal applications or recruitment consultancies. Even more astonishingly, only one in six managers heard about their job through close friends and family. The great majority of leads came from colleagues and casual acquaintances, with a quarter coming from a person whom the successful applicant hardly knew at all:

In many cases, the contact was only marginally included in the current network of contacts, such as an old college friend or a former workmate or employer . . . Usually such ties had not even been very strong when first forged . . . Chance meetings or mutual friends operated to reactivate such ties. It is remarkable that people receive crucial information from individuals whose very existence they have forgotten.[4]

Granovetter speculated why friends and family – who are strongly motivated to help – are usually less valuable than casual acquaintances in our career turning points. He came to the conclusion that our friends, family and close colleagues form a 'closely knit clump of social structure' where most contacts are in touch with the others. These close contacts have access to the same information that we have, but not much more. So we have to move outside our immediate circle and contact the distant extremities of our social network to gain fresh insights and learn new information. This means renewing contacts with people from the past or cultivating new links with friends of friends.

This works especially well if you and your new contacts come from different backgrounds, do not share many mutual friends, work in contrasting occupations, and/or live far from each other simply because their contacts and knowledge will be very different from your own.

Red and green lottery tickets

Imagine that you can acquire an unlimited number of lottery tickets. Of course, the chance of winning the jackpot with any individual ticket is low, but the more tickets you collect, the greater is your chance of success. Now, imagine that the tickets are available in two colours, red and green. The red tickets are extremely expensive. You can 'buy' them only through putting in several years' hard work. So, for instance, you will get a single red ticket once you acquire a degree and another after amassing a considerable amount of work experience. These red tickets are the conventional, traditional route to success and no one is able to accumulate many of them during their lifetime. Moreover, despite their very high price, even winning red tickets tend to result in only modest prizes.

By contrast, the green tickets are cheap, sometimes almost free. Hundreds of them can be acquired without any hard work and they arrive quickly, often as a pleasant surprise, an unexpected windfall. They comprise information from casual acquaintances that we can turn to our advantage. Most of the time, these green tickets – just like the red ones – don't result in a jackpot . . . but a few of them do. For me, Nick Walt was one of my jackpot-winning green tickets. The minimal effort of walking to a wine bar turbo-charged my career.

In the game of *Monopoly*, a set of two or three properties of the *same* colour is much more valuable than four or five unrelated properties. But in life, a set of two *differently* coloured tickets, one red and one green, is the way to win. A good qualification or work experience – red ticket – may be invaluable, but so is the information – green ticket – that levers up your expertise. Given that the two colours have roughly the same value and chance of securing the jackpot, and that the green tickets are much cheaper than the red, it makes sense to acquire as many of the former as you can. This is the Principle in action.

I have hit the jackpot with several winning tickets during my lifetime:

- I gained a good undergraduate degree, which gave me confidence and marketability (red ticket), but I acquired it through very selective study (green ticket).
- I learned that two colleagues were contemplating starting a new consulting firm (green ticket), and joined them when they took the plunge.
- I met Nick Walt at Julie's Wine Bar and reaped the benefits over the next six years (green ticket).
- I made investments in five new or young firms based on information provided by acquaintances (green tickets), which again led to large returns.
- I met my current circle of close friends, as well as my partner, through acquaintances (green tickets).

As you can see, all but one of these winning tickets was green. If you compile your own list of life-changing events, you will probably get a similar result. You are much more likely to win with a green ticket (acquired through little or no effort) than with a red ticket (acquired through enormous effort), although it helps to have both if you are planning to scoop the jackpot.

You might like to think that the green tickets arrive through pure luck. That is almost true, except for the fact that you have to invest a little effort to get your hands on them, such as going out and meeting someone you hardly know. But remember, the more tickets you acquire, the more luck you will have, and green tickets are much easier to acquire than red. Typically, at least 99 per cent of our effort goes on acquiring those rare red tickets, even though they have no more chance of securing the jackpot. Meanwhile, we devote the remaining 1 per cent to acquiring hundreds of green tickets, every one of which might lead to most of what makes life rich and fun.

By now, you should have worked out exactly what to do: concentrate on extending your network of weak links both inside and, crucially, outside work so you acquire as many green tickets as possible. This will allow you to gain insights and information that your colleagues do not possess. Maintain a raft of distant but friendly acquaintances who have the potential to give a high payoff for very little effort on your part.

You have no way of knowing where any single contact might lead or how high its value might be. But eventually you are likely to win that life-changing jackpot because of one of them.

Superconnectors

It gets even better, though. By far the greatest benefits of weak links accrue to the few people who have the most personal contacts. This finding – an important one for successful managers to take on board – came from research conducted by one of America's greatest social psychologists, Stanley Milgram. In 1967 Milgram experimented to see how 'big' or 'small' the world really was. He was curious to learn whether people far away from each other, socially and geographically, could be reached through a series of weak links; and, if so, how many links were typically needed to connect them.

Milgram enlisted volunteers in Wichita, Kansas, and Omaha, Nebraska, to see if they could get a folder to a target person they didn't know who lived far away – in Cambridge, Massachusetts, and Boston, respectively. The volunteers had to post the folder to someone with whom they were on first-name terms and who might be 'closer' to the target person. (Milgram's studies were conducted long before the internet, email and online social networks.) This friend would then be invited to post the folder on to one of their friends or acquaintances, who would do the same, until either the chain broke or the folder reached the target person.

Milgram reasoned that if the folders made it all the way to the target person in a relatively short chain of contacts then we lived in a 'small world', where acquaintances can act as stepping-stones to anyone we want to reach. He and a colleague wrote, 'The phrase "small world" suggests that social networks are in some sense tightly woven, full of unexpected strands linking individuals far removed from one another in physical or social space.'[5] If the folders didn't get through, that would indicate a 'large world', where there are unbridgeable gaps between discrete groups of people because nobody has a foot in both camps. Similarly, if the folders reached the target person eventually but through a very large number of links, the world could still be viewed as 'large', because the links would be so inefficient as to be unusable.

The results vindicated the 'small world' thesis. In the Nebraska study, 160 chains were started and 44 completed. The number of links in the chains varied between two and ten, with the average five – much lower than the researchers expected. Eerily, this is precisely the number guessed by a character in a short story called 'Chain Links', published in 1929. The Hungarian author, Frigyes Karinthy, wrote, 'To demonstrate that people on Earth are much closer than ever, a member of the group suggested a test. He bet that we could name any person amongst Earth's one and a half billion inhabitants, and through at most five acquaintances, one of whom he knew personally, he could link to the target person.'[6] The idea was later adopted by John Guare for his play *Six Degrees of Separation*, which was subsequently turned into a Hollywood movie. Later research using emails and instant-message communications showed results that averaged between five and seven links. This is a truly remarkable case of scientific research vindicating popular American folklore derived ultimately from a forgotten Hungarian writer – in itself a demonstration in miniature of the 'small world' in action.

For managers, Milgram's most telling finding concerns the identities of the most popular links. In another of his 'send the folder' experiments, the target individual was a stockbroker who worked in Boston but lived in the suburb of Sharon, Massachusetts. Of the forty-four folders he received, no fewer than sixteen of them came via one final 'funnel', a shopkeeper called 'Mr Jacobs' (a pseudonym) who sold clothes in Sharon. The stockbroker, Milgram reported, was 'shocked' at how many of the folders came through Jacobs. Milgram called Jacobs a 'sociometric star'. The small world exists only because a relatively small number of people – like Jacobs – form most of the links between the rest of us.[7]

In addition to the sixteen folders the target received from Jacobs, a further ten came from 'Mr Jones' and five more from 'Mr Brown', both of whom were fellow stockbrokers. Without these three final links in the chain, nearly half of the folders may not have reached the target and the world would not have seemed so small.

We have seen something very similar to this pattern before.

An impressive 25 per cent (16 out of 64) of the folders arrived through just 1.6 per cent (1 out of 64) of the final links; and 48 per cent (31 out of 64) came from just 4.7 per cent (3 out of 64) of the final links. We saw earlier that the 80/20 Principle has two very close cousins – the 50/5 principle and the 20/1 principle. If 80 per cent of results come from 20 per cent of the total, 50 per cent of results may come from 5 per cent of the total, and 20 per cent from as little as 1 per cent of the total. That is almost exactly what we see with Milgram's 'stars'. The small world depends on a small minority of people who have many more social – and usually weak – links than the majority. I prefer to call these people 'superconnectors'.

Crucially, these superconnectors use each of their weak links much more frequently than the majority use theirs. They have access to many times more information than most people. They hear news first – not from the mass media, which inform tens of millions of people simultaneously, but from their own proprietary and unique networks of friendly acquaintances, who filter the 'news' to generate items of particular interest to the superconnector. As a result, superconnectors lead far richer lives than most people.

Links within a firm will be 'denser clumps of social structure' – tangled together and introverted. The bigger the firm, the more internal permutations there will be, and the more likely its managers will be to neglect or undervalue external links.

Does that describe you?

Make a list of all your friendly acquaintances – people with whom you are on first-name terms and whose company you enjoy – inside the firm. Now list all of your friendly acquaintances *outside* the firm. You will speak to these people professionally from time to time and they will provide information and insights that are relevant, either directly or indirectly, to your work. They may be former workmates, customers, suppliers, consultants, industry experts, friends or friends of friends – anyone with whom you can have a mutually rewarding discussion about some aspect of your work.

Compare the two lists. Which is longer? Which is higher

quality – more helpful in your daily work? Which is more diverse, with people from a wide variety of backgrounds and locations who have contrasting skill sets and attitudes?

If your external list is longer and more useful, congratulations, you are already a superconnector. If not, you have a great opportunity to become one.

How to become a superconnector

A superconnector links people from disparate backgrounds, acting as a bridge between people who would benefit from knowing each other, but don't. If you want to become a superconnecting manager, here's how to do it:

- Begin by improving your network of connections within the firm, especially with high-performing (80/20) managers and with 'diverse' links – executives who are dissimilar to you and those who work in other departments or distant locations. To increase your number of friendly acquaintances, be open and helpful whenever you first meet someone (and subsequently, of course). Initiate a face-to-face chat with at least one contact each week, ideally outside the office. The best conversations are spontaneous and personal, with no explicit agenda (or with one that can be quickly dispatched). Range far and wide. Be open about your life and work. Encourage the other person to ask for favours or insights. Ask them if they would like to meet any of your other contacts. Work out which of your weak links could be helpful to the other person and introduce them yourself.

- Use travel on work business to get to know your acquaintances better.
- Join cross-disciplinary and cross-location project teams.
- If you can, work overseas for a time. When you return home, retain contact with your overseas network. After a few years, go to a different country.
- Be willing to change firms even if you are feeling comfortable in your existing job, and then keep in touch with your former colleagues. Part of Silicon Valley's success derives from the extensive open contact it has engendered between colleagues and ex-colleagues. Managers there change firms on average every two years. When you change jobs, you automatically acquire a new network, but there's no need to lose your previous one. Your contacts will be much more numerous and valuable if you (and your former colleagues) change jobs frequently.
- Gravitate towards departments and jobs that require extensive external contact – for example, marketing or customer-facing roles.
- Form a dining club of external friendly acquaintances. Ensure the participants are dissimilar. Meet informally two or three times a year to discuss a provocative topic. You could even invite an external speaker to get the conversation going.

- Learn about new ideas by reading magazines, trade
  journals and books that nobody else in the firm (and
  especially your department) is likely to read. Take
  magical mystery tours online and explore parts of
  the internet that your colleagues never see. Be
  adventurous when you go on holiday by travelling to
  countries that your colleagues would never dream of
  visiting.

Fortunately, you don't have to be a bouncing extrovert or
a 'people person' to become a superconnector. Most
superconnectors are just open, approachable and friendly . . .
to everyone. Don't try to screen out people you think might
not be 'useful'. You have no way of knowing who is going
to be truly useful at some point in the future, and everyone
– from the dentist's receptionist, to the new employee in
your office, to your brother's partner – has their own story
to tell. I used to be somewhat reserved, but now I chat to
people standing next to me at the supermarket checkout,
to other dog walkers, to anyone with whom I share space
and time. You are either open, with a ready smile and a
listening ear, or you're not; you can't (or at least shouldn't)
switch it on or off. And once you are open to the world,
connecting people and ideas becomes second nature, and
life takes on numerous delightful new dimensions.

Building up a network of a few hundred friendly
acquaintances is not hard, even if you are shy. Everyone is
drawn to certain types of people, either because the
chemistry clicks or because they share common interests

or values. Every week, we all meet several new characters, whether through work, family or random encounters, and one or more of these can easily become a friendly acquaintance. We all have friends who have friends, and these friends of friends are easy to meet and get to know. Then there are those people in the background of your life – your sister's gardener, the florist, your local bartender, fellow worshippers at church – any one of whom you could choose to know better. You will also have several large latent networks of people from your past – school, college, former friends and colleagues, and former bosses.

The secret to superconnecting is to *use* all of those networks to *help* your contacts. So email one of your contacts and put them in touch with another whom they might be able to help. Do it now. The worst that can happen is that they ignore your email, and you might just start something great for both of them.

Humans have an inbuilt desire to collaborate and help each other. And that instinct becomes stronger with practice, as we build confidence in connecting individuals and garner ever more of the free insights that surround us, but which we rarely used to notice. In any case, don't worry about your own reward – it *will* come sooner or later, probably when you least expect it and from an unanticipated direction. And the great thing is that once you get into the swing of it, superconnecting is easy and fun – it becomes a way of life that will help you and your acquaintances enormously.

Connecting – and superconnecting – is especially beneficial for managers. That's because most companies tend to be inward-looking, and most managers spend more time talking to their colleagues within the firm than to people outside it. Internal communication can be useful but it has its limits. As Mark Granovetter discovered, a single pool of ideas and insights is shared by most of the managers in a firm, so fresh ideas are much more likely to come from outside, from different sources of information and inspiration. It follows that those managers who cultivate weak links outside the firm will come across many more of these good ideas and useful contacts.

Even within the firm, especially if it is large and complex, connecting previously unconnected fellow managers who are engaged in different activities might reap rich rewards. Managers who form these bridges are naturally more knowledgeable and creative than those who don't take the trouble to make connections. These bridge-builders are better placed to spot opportunities that other managers miss. Every new business starts by juxtaposing new and old ideas, and managers can play this game just as well as entrepreneurs, with less risk and greater resources at their disposal.

How does the idea of superconnecting relate to the 80/20 Principle? The Canadian singer Michael Bublé co-wrote a song in 2009 called 'Haven't Met You Yet' which features the charming idea that the most important person in our lives is yet to be met. The theory of superconnecting tells us that it is only by meeting a wide range of disparate people that we can discover the person or people, or idea or ideas, that could change our lives. Experimentation, in other words, is not the opposite of focus; it is a necessary precursor to it.

We have seen how the Principle can be used to improve the efficiency of a business through investigation; and how bringing together disparate ideas and people can greatly increase your chances of winning the work jackpot. Now it's time to explore a third way that can also lead to vastly superior management performance. Once again, it is relatively easy to master, deeply satisfying, yet bafflingly neglected: mentoring.

Way Three: The Mentoring Manager

Knowledge is like money: to be of value, it must circulate.

Louis L'Amour

It is a human trait to want to pass on wisdom.

Jack Canfield[1]

'Mentoring' and 'being mentored' are just fancy terms for teaching and learning. Except that both can be very personal. Look back on all the jobs you've had – including different jobs in the same firm – and ask what you learned in each job, and how. Chances are that your most valuable lessons came from a boss or colleague.

That's certainly true for me. My first job as a junior manager was in a Shell oil refinery. I loathed it, but I learned one thing, from one person. A guy called Dan Rawlinson was a fan of Peter Drucker, perhaps the best management writer. Dan transformed the refinery by introducing a programme of 'Management by Objectives', based on Drucker's philosophy (which, incidentally, I think is due for a revival). Drucker proposed that each manager should: write a short list of his or her objectives for the year, focusing on those that would generate the most potent results; get the objectives approved by their boss; and be judged simply and entirely by whether they achieved the specified results. Dan taught me the importance of thinking in terms of *results*, not activities. As soon as I grasped that idea, I left.

I moved to a pet-food business owned by the Mars brothers, where I assumed responsibility for their annual pay survey of local firms. However, very few of these companies responded to my questionnaire so I was forced to tell my boss, a dynamic Scot named David Drennan, that the survey was useless. He was not impressed and told me to call the non-respondents' human resources departments, go to see them, and do anything I could to find out their pay rates. After some trepidation, I ended up having a lot of fun visiting people and getting their data. We ended up with the most comprehensive survey in the company's history. David showed me what was possible by lighting a bomb under me, and since then I have taught countless young people the same lesson.

A good friend of mine, the bestselling author of *The Dream Manager*, Matthew Kelly, says that most people want a mentoring manager, even if they don't admit it. He tells the following inspirational story from his time as a consultant to a large manufacturing company.

Matthew Kelly's story[2]

My task was to improve the productivity of several plants. I assembled a team of seven managers working for the client so the work could be sustained after I left. We travelled from plant to plant for two weeks before setting up a war room at the company headquarters.

There must be something about consultants. Maybe we dress or smell differently, because when we talk to employees they say things that unlock problems before our eyes. We heard two things over and over. The heads of the plants asked us, 'What have we done wrong? The only time anyone comes from HQ is when we've done something wrong.' Meanwhile, on the shop floor, there were many comments along these lines: 'I've been here twenty years and you're the first person from HQ who's ever spoken to me.'

I shared these comments with the team, but they just shrugged. They were more comfortable discussing technical issues, such as the workflow of the plants or the supply chain. The next month we spent two weeks making adjustments to the workflow in one plant. Productivity there in the next quarter rose by 12 per cent. We went back to focus on workspace and equipment. During the next quarter, productivity climbed by another 9 per cent.

We did this in nine plants over the year. The results were

unquestionable. Some were better than others, but in every case the client was delighted. They wrote my firm a large cheque, shook my hand, and said, 'We can take it from here.' Throughout the project, I had kept trying to bring them back to the things their people had said to us during our first visits. But they didn't want to go there.

Eighteen months later, my phone rang. The client needed me back. A new project? No. The old project. After we had finished, productivity in all nine plants had slid back to the original level. And now it was *below* where we started.

I asked the CEO the simple questions consultants are paid a fortune to ask.

'What has changed?'

'Nothing.'

'Did you undo anything we implemented?'

'No.'

'Is there a new competitor on the scene?'

'No.'

'Is the equipment being maintained regularly?'

'Yes.'

'How is morale among the workers at the plants?'

'I don't know.'

Seriously, that's what he said to me. So I asked, 'When was the last time you were at one of the nine plants?'

'I'm not sure.'

I encouraged him to guess.

'Maybe nine months ago.'

The truth is, I knew what his answers would be before I asked the questions.

When the project team was in the plants, talking to line workers and managers, enquiring about their work, listening to the stories of their lives, asking what could be done to help them do their jobs better, the energy level was incredible. You could feel the difference between the first day we visited and when we were working there.

What was the difference?

We were taking an interest in them.

People are people are people. Develop a basic understanding of the human person or you will fail. And one of the main drivers in every human being is this: when people take an interest in us, we thrive.

The mentoring manager takes an interest in his or her people.

When we were working in those plants, we were taking an interest. The technical changes were good but they had a minor impact. The real change was in the people.

So when we went back into the plants for the second time, we got the folks from head office to listen to what the line workers and managers were saying, to form links within the plants and between them, to develop project teams comprising line operatives to improve performance across plants, and to circulate workers between them. We also organized mentoring programmes. That way we achieved the technical improvements again, but we also tapped the energy, ideas and motivation of the people in the plants, so that outside consultants would never be necessary again and the productivity gains could become a way of life.

Everyone yearns for others to pay attention to them and their work. No matter how young or old we are, how interesting or repetitive our work, or our level of education, we all want to have interest taken in us and our work. Tragically, though, while we all yearn for this, most people don't receive genuine care and curiosity and support. And that's before we even venture an interest in the personal and professional development of a person.

Nobody excels without a coach or mentor, even if they are not called that. Sure, you can take yourself a certain distance on your own. But to excel, and sustain high performance, humans need coaches and mentors. In the last forty years, not a single athlete has attended the summer Olympic Games without a coach. Why? Well, coaches provide experience and ideas, and they make you accountable. But perhaps most of all they give encouragement.

Who is encouraging your people? If it's not you, it's probably not happening. If it's not happening, your team is miles from achieving all it could.

And encouraging your people is just one part of being a mentoring manager.

Most managers get the job they are doing now because they did their last job well. But that doesn't mean they will be good managers, and generally they are not. Too many people think that when they become a manager, it's all about them now. The exact opposite is true. The day we make manager, it's no longer about us; it's about the people we serve as a manager.

You may have been great at your last job. But how many

high-profile sporting stars do we see retiring and taking a coaching job, only to fail miserably? You won't necessarily be a good coach just because you were a great player.

Anyone can put together a budget or strategy document, but the real work needs to be done with people. For all the technology advances in the last fifty years, business is still about people. On both sides of every business transaction you find people. And people are the toughest part of any business. You'll lay awake at night thinking about people problems more than you will about numbers or strategy.

I've been tremendously fortunate throughout my life to have a string of fabulous mentors. The difference for me has been the steady stream of people who took the time to take an interest in me. My parents began that; my older brothers carried it on. My first boss, when I was just twelve, took an exceptional interest in my development. A long line of incredible schoolteachers, coaches for soccer, tennis, swimming, cricket, golf – they all took an interest. They all encouraged me.

So the question to answer is this: are you willing to invest in *your* people?

Their growth matters more than marketing, strategy, finance, technical skills, industry knowledge or customer intimacy. If you don't believe it now, you'll learn this lesson at a high cost.

The best people, in particular, are always looking for a mentor. They want to hear about your successes, but they will learn plenty from your failures, too.

A couple of years ago, I heard a top executive from

Procter & Gamble speaking to a group. I was intrigued that he chose to talk about the worst time in his career. (Not many people broadcast their blunders.) He had pushed his team to implement a price increase when some of the indicators suggested they should not. Most of his people were opposed to the new price, but he overruled them. Before long, they were losing market share hand over fist.

Still, the executive had the courage to gather his team together and admit his mistake. 'I was wrong,' he said. 'Several of you tried to talk sense to me. I didn't listen. I'm sorry.' Then he asked the team to redouble their efforts to fix the problem. He made no attempt to hide the scale of the task: it would be an enormous job for a division of their size.

His people didn't hesitate. They got stuck into it with terrific energy and resolution. Within two years they had recaptured their previous market share. Then they surpassed it and came to dominate the sector.

Do you think the boss lost respect by admitting his error? No, he gained it in spades. When we make ourselves vulnerable, we give people permission to be human. And that humanity encourages them to help us recover and succeed again.

So, you should never present yourself as infallible. Share your successes, but be open about your failures, too. Think back over your career, and you will discover that your best bosses were invariably mentoring managers. They took an interest in you and in all the other people they led. They were committed to encouraging people. And they were frank and honest not only about what worked for them but also about what did not.

How to become a mentoring manager

I hope Matthew's words inspire you to become a mentoring manager yourself. You will have to invest some effort and determination to make it happen, but rest assured, the results will be well worth it. Mentoring will improve the health of your organization, multiply the talents of your people, enhance your own humanity, and increase the pleasure you get from work.

Here are some of the ways in which the 80/20 Principle applies to mentoring:

- Fewer than 20 per cent of managers are effective mentors, yet this small group of leaders probably account for more than 80 per cent of the performance difference attributable to the human factor. That's hugely significant!
- Mentoring is a great example of how a small amount of energy can produce amazing results. Because people yearn for attention, direction and encouragement, a few minutes of your time can keep them motivated throughout the working week. Mentoring is a quintessentially 80/20 activity – it is incredibly leveraged. You get a massive bang for your invested buck. People think of mentoring as a big job. They're right in one respect, because it does

have a terrific impact. But they're wrong if they believe that it is a huge, time-consuming undertaking. Five minutes here and there, at the appropriate time and with the correct levels of empathy and intensity, can make all the difference.

- You are likely to achieve the best mentoring results through the least effort if you tell your people about the Principle and the ten ways to become a super-effective manager. But don't spout theory at them. Wait until one of the ten ways has worked wonders for you, then tell them about it. Share how easy (or hard) it was to master, and let them know about the satisfaction you get from being on top of your workload. Discuss with each person which of the ten ways they should tackle first. Ask how they plan to start – which practical steps will they take? Then, each week, ask them how it's going. If it's not working, spend a few minutes there and then putting them back on track. If you help just one of your colleagues to become an 80/20 manager, you will multiply their value for life.

- Get everyone you mentor to agree to mentor at least two other people in the firm. If the people they mentor then do the same, you will soon build a mountain of mentors. And, of course, the impact will be even more profound if you teach your 'sub-mentors' to use the ten ways with the colleagues they help.

- Make raising the performance of the people they

mentor an important part of performance appraisal for your managers. In fact, try to get this included in the firm-wide system. If you can't do that officially, do it informally. Whenever you discuss performance with one of your people, touch on the performance of the people they are mentoring, too. If there has not been a dramatic improvement, suggest that the mentor needs to ask him- or herself why. They need to acknowledge what they are failing to do, or what they are doing ineffectively.

- The Principle suggests that there will be only a few really great mentors in any firm, and their results will put most other mentors in the shade. So, identify the great mentors and analyse precisely what they do. If you can't figure it out, ask them directly. If your enquiry is genuine, they'll be flattered and/or impressed. Once they've told you their secret, imitate them.

- Not everyone will be equally receptive. Everyone likes attention, but not everyone will get the message. It's not just about feeling appreciated; it's about starting to achieve extraordinary results. Three groups tend to benefit most from mentoring: those who thirst for hints on how to raise their game; managers who are already doing well; and those who know they are floundering. For the people doing well, train them to focus on their existing power alleys so that their skills become truly world class. Encourage them to deploy their full personalities, their quirks and passions, and bake those into the way they excel. For those who are floundering, you need to catch them doing *something* right and praise it. This will turn a flickering flame into a fountain of light. Everyone does something really well, it's just a case of recognizing what it is. You also need to identify the *few* things they do that are most harmful to both themselves and their colleagues. Then offer advice on how to eliminate or improve them. It's much easier to stop making a few mistakes than to achieve a general improvement across the board.

- Because these three groups – those who crave mentoring; those who are already performing well; and those who are doing badly – will reap the greatest benefits from intensive mentoring, you should put most of your effort into helping them. In most cases, this will still consume mere fragments of your time, but it's vital to care about these individuals and their performance. If you care, your sixth sense will tell you when and where you should spend a few moments intervening. If you don't care, mentoring becomes a chore, no more than an item on your checklist, and you'll do more harm than good. People are not idiots. They know when you are just going through the motions. The way to great mentoring is to care about your people.
- Some of your interventions will work better than others. This might be due to you feeling more inspirational on some days than others. But it is

more likely to be a case of your intervention coinciding with when your colleague feels most in need of help, direction or a simple morale boost. So, if you want to make the best use of your time and energy, pick up on the small signals people send out when they need your advice, care and guidance.

How to find great mentoring

Mentoring is an 80/20 activity, but so is being mentored. It doesn't matter who you are – the lowliest clerk, the CEO of a multinational corporation, or the President of the United States – we all need support and coaching. We all need mentors. Who are yours? If you can't think of any, do something about it right away.

Here are some tips for acquiring and retaining a really good mentor:

- Go for quality over quantity. One terrific mentor is worth five very good ones.
- Don't be afraid to ask the person you really want to mentor you, even if they are important and busy and there's no obvious reason why they should agree. As Jack Canfield writes, 'successful people like to share what they have learned with others . . . Not everyone will take the time to mentor you, but many will if asked.'[3] Don't confine yourself to your firm, industry or country. Distance mentoring works surprisingly well.

- Once you've found your mentor, don't demand too much of their time. Make the whole process as easy as possible for them. But don't shy away from asking for help when you need it most. Every good mentor knows what they are there for; and they will be disappointed if you don't ask for help at a critical time.

- Listen intently. The best mentors may not spell out what they mean. Few people like to be brutally honest, so learn to read between the lines. Or ask them to elaborate.

- The best advice is useless unless you act upon it. Put the counsel to work *immediately*.

- If your mentor is helping you become a super-effective manager, integrate their advice into whichever of the ten ways you have chosen to master. Actions are much more potent when they're in context – a focused striving after specific results, rather than miscellaneous aspirations. So tell your mentor about the ten ways and the one you have selected. This may even help them to become a more effective manager (and mentor)!

- Give something back. I am currently mentoring an Australian in his twenties, Luke Stone, who contacted me after reading my books. After our first conversation, he sent me two terrific DVDs of inspirational speakers. Then, a week ago, he followed this up by sending me Jack Canfield's book, *The Success Principles* (from which I've just quoted). I thought I knew all of that material, but I was wrong. Luke introduced me to some angles I would never have found on my own.

Mentoring the 80/20 way

Mentoring and being mentored are truly 80/20 activities because they are highly enjoyable and satisfying while also providing enormous rewards for very little investment in time and effort. Business is a social activity, and success in business is driven by ideas and vision. By sharing and receiving insights, and giving and receiving support when it is most needed, you can lift your game (and those of friends and colleagues) to new heights. That makes mentoring not only one of the easiest of the ten ways, but one of the sweetest. How strange, then, that it is usually so neglected.

Which of the three ways presented so far – investigating, superconnecting and mentoring – do you think most fits your personality and aspirations? Consider each of them carefully. But don't make a decision just yet, because there's a fourth relatively easy way to extraordinary results: becoming a leveraged manager.

Way Four: The Leveraged Manager

Give me a place to stand, and with a lever I
will move the whole world.

Archimedes

You may not be able to move the globe with a lever bought
from your local hardware store, but such a lever will
certainly allow you to move a large paving stone without
breaking a sweat. In this chapter, we will look at seven
levers that managers can use to magnify their impact. Some
of the ideas might appear a little left-field, but they all
work.

The value of levers is well illustrated by the main
protagonist in Donna Leon's delightfully evocative murder
mystery books.

Commissario Guido Brunetti is a most unusual detective.
At ten in the morning, he can often be found enjoying an
espresso – chased down by a small brandy – in a bar near

Venice's main police station. Typically, he walks home for a full lunch, during which he shares a decent bottle of wine with his wife Paola, a professor. After conducting a little light investigation in the afternoon, always pausing to soak up the local atmosphere, he is back home at a civilized hour for dinner and more stimulating conversation with Paola and their two children.

But despite his drinking, Brunetti is effective. He solves even the most impenetrable murder cases – including some to which he is not even assigned – although, naturally, it always takes him three hundred pages to do so.

How does he do it? Like all good 80/20 managers, he thinks a great deal before he acts. He rejects the obvious answers and puzzles over the few significant issues that seem to make no sense. (These cogitations are often the most discursive, fascinating and surprising sections of the novels.) So far, so typical of a modern fictional detective. But the commissario also has a lever that is not available to any of his colleagues, for Guido is the only policeman who understands the mysterious powers of his boss's secretary, Signorina Elettra, who can hack into almost any database in Italy. In *A Question of Belief*, for example, Guido, to whom cyberspace is a complete mystery, receives invaluable information from Elettra that helps him crack the case. In fact, she is the lever in all of the recent Brunetti novels, allowing Guido to achieve results out of all proportion to the effort he commits to a case.

Of course, leverage is not just a great device for thriller writers. It is equally useful for 80/20 managers. I'm not suggesting that you should go hacking into computers; leave that to the media or the police. But you should exploit as many levers as you can. By 'lever', I mean any simple device that has the power to multiply the effectiveness of your input and so allows you to achieve extraordinary results through ordinary effort.

Seven levers for great results

1. Caring and the power of the subconscious
2. Confidence
3. Ideas
4. Decisions
5. Trust
6. People
7. Money

Caring and the power of the subconscious

Caring and engagement are so obvious that their impact is often overlooked. When we don't really care, we miss vital clues that might lead to breakthroughs. Caring – deep caring, where we have a determination to achieve a goal – operates constantly, working in the background when our minds are elsewhere. You have probably experienced an idea popping into your head, seemingly from nowhere. But that happens only when you truly care about something.

Experiments have proved that conscious thought is most effective when there are no more than a few bits of data to piece together – for example, I look at a map, see two viable routes, and choose one of them.[1] The subconscious is better for solving all of the really interesting problems, when the information is ambiguous, tangled, complex and confusing in its profusion. This is when we need to process multiple streams of evidence and impressions from many separate and contradictory sources, using information from all of our senses and emotion as well as reason.

For example, rational thought is unable to tell you whether to start (or end) an intimate personal relationship, but the subconscious can. It works by churning over any problem that is important to us, operating slowly but surely, before eventually flooding our conscious mind with solutions when we least expect them. The philosopher Bertrand Russell had one of his greatest conceptual breakthroughs while buying a tin of pipe tobacco. Henri Poincaré, the great French mathematician, solved a highly complex problem that had defeated him for years while boarding a bus and talking to a friend about something completely different.

The subconscious fits perfectly into the 80/20 Principle. It is extremely economical because it works away for free on your behalf while you concentrate on other, more mundane tasks. It provides fresh, creative and quirky ideas that wouldn't surface if you were reliant on your plodding, linear thought processes. Yet most managers don't make full use of their subconscious lever because they don't care enough about the problems it tackles.

Have you ever heard of someone waking up in the middle of the night with an exciting new perspective on something that didn't truly interest them? How marvellous, though, when the subconscious reconciles the irreconcilable, supplies the missing piece of the jigsaw puzzle, transcends your conscious thinking to find a beautiful and utterly unexpected explanation for a seemingly intractable problem. If you have ever experienced that feeling, you will know that it's an almost mystical – and highly pleasurable – sensation.

So, how much do you *really* care about your work and your company, on a scale of one to ten? Be honest. Now compare your answer with other aspects of your life. If you are a parent with young children, you will probably give them a ten. Your health or love life may be a nine or a ten, too. If you don't give your objectives at work a similarly high score, you don't really care about them. Most managers rate work at between six and eight, which is not enough to get the subconscious motoring, unpaid and unseen, so they will not benefit from the extraordinary results it can achieve through minimal effort.

Caring generates its own energy. When he was getting on in years, the great choreographer George Balanchine said, 'I've got more energy than when I was younger, because I know exactly what I want to do.' He cared about one very specific thing – becoming the best choreographer he could be. Caring is also closely related to meaning, which in turn leads to happiness. Your life has meaning if you care passionately about something, and none if you don't. If you don't care about something that takes up half your waking hours, you are half dead. You are only half as happy as you could be.

If, like most people, you gave your job as a whole a score

of six, seven or eight, try to identify one small, individual aspect of your work life that means more (a nine or a ten) to you. Could you change jobs within the firm in order to spend all your time on that? Even if there is no such position at the moment, perhaps you could persuade your bosses that there should be. If something small in your professional life currently accounts for 80 per cent or more of your professional passion, try to make it 100 per cent of what you do. Think of how much more fun you will have and how much more effective you will be.

Now you can start to make full use of your fantastic subconscious thought processor. Keep it well fed, so it's always chugging away in the background. As soon as it solves one complex problem – something, of course, about which you care deeply – send it another. This becomes a virtuous circle, ensuring that you always care about *something*, and it continues to operate without any effort whatsoever.

When I was a student, I was told to read all of the exam questions carefully before starting to write my first answer. This gave my subconscious the opportunity to begin to marshal information for all of the answers. Similarly, it's a good idea to write down a list of half a dozen questions for your subconscious right now, so it can get to work on them. That way, there will be no delay in moving on to the next question once the first is solved.

The subconscious, then, can be a terrific lever, but only if you care passionately about achieving your objectives at work. If you are not interested, it will be similarly apathetic.

Confidence

Leverage also comes from confidence. It helps you achieve what others don't even attempt.

There's a true story about a handful of soldiers who got lost on a training exercise in the Alps when they became detached from their battalion. The snow disoriented them. Every peak looked the same. They argued about which way to go. Light was fading. They were cold, hungry and afraid. They had little chance of surviving the night in the freezing temperatures. Then a miracle happened. One of them found a map in the lining of his kitbag. He figured out the route, pointed the way, and they all marched briskly back to base. It was only when they were warm and well fed that the soldier looked closer at the map. It was of the Pyrenees, hundreds of miles away.

Another amazing, true story comes from the development of the first easy-to-use computer. In December 1979, Steve Jobs and his chief product engineer, Bill Atkinson, were blown away by a visit to Xerox PARC, where they glimpsed all the features of a new generation of PCs, including a desktop, icons, a mouse, a graphical user interface and 'windows' to organize similar files and programs. Walking away from the Xerox research facility, Atkinson was particularly taken with the idea (which, of course, we take for granted today) that the windows overlapped seamlessly, so that the page you were reading followed directly from the page above and would lead to the page below. This was something that no computer had previously been able to accomplish because, although it was a simple idea, it was incredibly hard to realize. Nevertheless, Atkinson reckoned that if the scientists at Xerox could do it, then, given enough time and effort, his team could too. And they did.

The only thing was that the Xerox team had never actually achieved this. They were in awe when they saw Atkinson's overlapping windows, because it was the holy grail that had always eluded them. Atkinson attributed his success to 'the empowering aspect of naiveté . . . because I didn't know it couldn't be done, I was enabled to do it'.[2] There was a little more to it than that: he was able to do it because he was confident it had already been done.

Confidence has the power to generate a super-positive force-field, life-saving energy, impossibility-defying ingenuity. It allows us to experience elation and infectious passion. It confers vigour and the ability to seize opportunities that would otherwise seem impossible, or might not even be noticed.

Assurance comes from visualizing success. See yourself winning – then do so. If you are unable to imagine success at a very high level, lower the bar. If you can't run uphill, run where it's flat. It's the winning that's important. Even modest achievements will breed confidence that will help you go higher next time. Set goals that you are confident you can achieve. Because confidence makes life easy, while a lack of confidence makes everything hard or even impossible, it follows that you must be confident to achieve great results through ordinary effort. So experiment with different jobs until you discover your 'field of confidence'.

Ideas

Every business starts with an idea. And if the business is to thrive, that idea has to be a good one. But every idea can be improved. Unless it dies, any product or service will inevitably change and become better. Before that can happen, though, there has to be a different or better idea.

This cycle strongly resembles what happens in nature. We can trace evolution by natural selection in every business. Millions of new business ideas surface every year, but very few of them survive long enough to become a new product or service. The few ideas that fit best in their respective markets survive, but not for long. Why? Because better ideas for better products replace them. Business is a highly accelerated process of natural selection. Species evolve over millions of years. New products come to full maturity over years or even months. Species die out over millions of years. Products die over years or months.

Evolution is the 80/20 Principle operating over time. The great economist Joseph Schumpeter called this process 'creative destruction', a phrase that Charles Darwin could equally have coined. Nature exhibits creative destruction and so does business. In nature, it operates through genes, which mutate randomly and generate both worse and better versions of themselves. In this sense, 'better' means more likely to survive in their environment. Fitter species destroy less fit ones. In business, creative destruction operates through ideas for new businesses and products. Each idea generates a product that encapsulates itself and allows it to be distributed widely, just as genes create creatures to house and propagate themselves.

Take transportation as an example. Back in the Stone Age, the only way to travel was to walk or run. There was no 'transportation business'. Then a market in travel slowly emerged. About four thousand years before Christ, someone in Central Asia had the bright idea of taming horses and riding on their backs. Initially, the horses were small and could carry only children or very small adults. Then someone else thought: why not breed bigger horses that will be able to carry adults and freight? A new product was evolved: the large horse. Later ideas created new markets for horses: horse-drawn ploughs, warhorses, racing horses for gambling, and so on. As new ideas created larger and more diverse markets, the world's horse population exploded to meet the demand. Roll history forward another two millennia, and someone came up with another bright idea: the chariot. Eventually, this evolved into the four-wheeled carriage pulled by teams of horses.

Then, in the nineteenth century, the *velocipede* ('fast foot' – the forerunner of the bicycle) appeared in France. This paved the way for the next wave of transport innovation. Cyclists lobbied for new and better roads, which in turn encouraged the development of a new, faster and more sophisticated machine – the motor car. In 1885, in Mannheim, Germany, Karl Benz built the first car to be powered by a petrol engine. Just over two decades later, in 1908, Henry Ford vowed to 'democratize the automobile' via a much cheaper, standardized car design. Since then, we have seen a proliferation of better, cheaper and more powerful cars, as well as trucks, vans, pick-up trucks, minivans, sports cars, sport-utility vehicles, motorbikes and scooters, not to mention other forms of transportation such as steamships, powerboats, supertankers, airplanes and many others.

Each of these new or improved transport machines began with an idea. And as the ideas multiplied, so did production and sales. Fantastically successful products, such as the Model T Ford, sold in their tens of millions . . . but then they were killed off by superior designs, just like all the rest.

Ideas are the ultimate source of human leverage. They have allowed us to conquer nature, liberating us from hunger, early death and isolation. The modern age is defined by the accelerating profusion of ever more useful ideas, embodied in far better and cheaper products.

Throughout history, though, a few ideas have been much more useful than the rest. The trick is to identify these *80/20 ideas*, all of which deliver much more for much less – more performance, comfort, satisfaction and delight for less energy, money, labour and time invested.

So, how do you do this?

- Remember that there is always a *much* better way of doing something. If the idea isn't many times better than existing ideas, find one that is. For example, in the 1950s and 1960s, computers were massive installations housed in rooms the size of a football pitch for temperature control.

Improvements were made year by year, but when I started work, in the early 1970s, computers were still far too expensive to be owned or used by individual managers. No chief executive anywhere on earth had a computer on his desk. It was the invention in 1975 of the microprocessor – a single chip that contained circuitry previously requiring huge cabinets – that made the personal computer a possibility. If scientists had been satisfied with making marginal improvements to the computer – rather than inventing something hundreds of times smaller and cheaper – you and I would not be using personal computers today. So, whenever you seek improvement, aim for something that is at least ten times better than what is available today.

- Take an existing successful idea and apply it in a different context. There is always a time lag. The steam engine transformed cotton mills in the 1770s, but it was another forty years or so before steamships emerged, then another three-quarters of a century before the technology was adapted in the production of cars. Things move faster now, but not as fast as you might think, even in 'leading-edge' sectors. Internet service providers emerged in the late 1980s and by 1995 the Internet was clearly entering the mainstream. Yet, almost two decades on, new online ideas still emerge from nowhere each year. The Internet, of course, is itself an 80/20 idea, delivering great new experiences and businesses out of all proportion to the resources needed to fund and run them. And there are many more applications of it that nobody has dreamed up, as yet.

- Apply a successful idea from one country or region to another. Red Bull claims to be the world's first energy drink. But how true is that? In 1962, an Austrian marketing manager, Dietrich Mateschitz, was on a routine business trip to Thailand. He noticed that the bicycle-taxi cyclists all drank the same soft drink while they were pedalling. That drink was Krating Daeng, which means Red Bull in English. Mateschitz is now apparently the richest person in Austria.
- Blend two successful ideas together: the wheel and the horse; a specialist hamburger restaurant and franchising (McDonald's); the tape recorder and portable radio (Sony Walkman); the Walkman and internet downloads (iPod). Don't try to reinvent the wheel – just merge it with another great idea.

Of course, not all ideas will be breakthroughs on this scale. Every 80/20 manager can use ideas, even relatively modest ones, to achieve ten- or twentyfold improvements in performance. That may seem unreasonably ambitious, but I promise you, those ideas are out there somewhere. They already exist. All you need to do is find them.

Decisions

Does a rabbit decide to excavate a burrow? Imagine Bugs Bunny behind a boardroom table debating with his advisers whether to go ahead. Of course, Bugs doesn't need a position paper on the burrow project. He acts on instinct. Only humans make conscious decisions, and they are great levers. Without decisions, we drift rudderless on the sea of life. With decisions, we summon up the crazy resolution to change the world around us. If we are decisive, we might well succeed. If we are indecisive, we never will.

Nowadays, we make more decisions than our forebears did. And the more senior you become, the more decisions you make.

Exert leverage by making firm decisions, especially those that are counter-intuitive, unprecedented or courageous. These are the 80/20 decisions:

- Counter-intuitive decisions. Trust the 80/20 Principle and put it into practice. Make decisions on the basis that relatively small expenditure of energy (or people, or money, or time) yields disproportionately impressive benefits. For example, if you eat five units of fruit and vegetables a day, your health will improve significantly at almost no cost. The same Principle applies if you exercise for thirty minutes a day. At work, a day and evening each week free from emails and mobile devices will raise your performance for negative effort.
- Unprecedented decisions. Take the plunge to decide

to do something nobody has ever tried before. Even if it proves to be a mistake, you might learn a lot or stumble across an unexpected opportunity. Christopher Columbus believed that the world was much smaller than was commonly believed. He calculated that the distance from Spain to Japan was only about 2300 miles, so he thought he could just about reach it without running out of food and water. By embarking on his famous trip, he gambled with his own and his sailors' lives. We now know that the correct distance, even if navigated in a perfect circle, is 7500 miles. Columbus and his crew had no chance of making it alive. Happily, just as their supplies started to run out, they landed in the Bahamas. When was the last time you made a decision to do something completely different – to live in a foreign country, change your career, learn a new discipline, or take your business in a completely new direction?

- Courageous decisions. Sometimes you need courage to make the right decision, especially if everyone else is telling you what a huge mistake you are making. For example, Winston Churchill stood almost alone in the mid-1930s when warning of the threat Hitler posed to world peace. He was either ignored or ridiculed, but his stalwart opposition to appeasement meant that he was eventually the only choice to lead the fight against the Nazis. Similarly, if you decide to embark on a project that has been dismissed as impossible by everyone else, it could make your career if you succeed and give you enormous leverage in the future. Of course, you must think very carefully before making this sort of decision and be certain that you are right.

We all make hundreds of decisions every day, but nearly all of them are trivial. Whether we order a Dell or Compaq computer, or have the Christmas party at a restaurant or a wine bar, matters little. According to the 80/20 Principle, all but a very few vital decisions should be made as far down the firm hierarchy as possible. So the next time the thorny issue of where to hold the Christmas party comes up, delegate the arrangements to the most junior (but still competent) person you can find. They will love the responsibility and you will save yourself a time-consuming headache.

No matter how senior you are, most of your decisions will make very little difference. If you don't believe me, make a list of all the decisions you make at work over the course of a single day. I bet that fewer than 10 per cent are of any consequence. Therefore, you should reduce the number of business decisions you make by at least 90 per cent, and probably by 99 per cent. If your firm demands that you, personally, must make certain decisions, identify and deal with the trivial ones as quickly as possible. Spend more time on the few truly vital decisions, especially those that demand courage and determination. An hour before you plan to go home each day, think of one vital decision that you haven't yet considered, the more important the better. Take that decision. Then go home.

Decisions are great levers. They are 80/20 devices because one good decision, reached after perhaps an hour of serious contemplation, might save months or even years of hard labour. Yet, most decisions do not fall into this category. They are inconsequential, trivial. So focus on taking the few crucial decisions, those that could transform your business and your life, and let the rest go hang.

Trust

Every manager knows what happens when you don't trust an employee. You don't give them important tasks or responsibility. Their output is low but your input is high because you are always checking up on them. You put in eighty units of effort for twenty units of reward.

But, of course, the opposite applies when you do trust a colleague. You give them challenging work that you would otherwise have to do yourself. Their output is high but your input is low because supervision is unnecessary. You get eighty units of reward for twenty units of effort, or maybe almost no effort at all.

Meanwhile, if your boss trusts you, you learn fast by working on the toughest assignments. Your job progressively comes to resemble that of your boss. Your expertise and value surge. You are no longer subjected to irksome supervision. You can focus on the few parts of your work where you achieve high returns for relatively little time and effort.

You can't become a great manager unless your boss trusts you and you trust your team. The essence of trust is that you focus on the outputs, not the inputs, and you allow your people to do the same. By contrast, when you don't trust someone, you judge them by inputs – have they done this, have they done that? So a lack of trust requires constant supervision, which makes it horrendously inefficient. It is the antithesis of the 80/20 approach. As a result, if you don't fully trust an individual, neither you nor they will be able to practise 80/20 management.

For managers who don't understand the Principle, trusting subordinates is desirable, because they know it is so much more efficient. But for 80/20 managers, trust is an absolute prerequisite. You simply cannot work without it. If you don't trust a member of your team, you need to move them elsewhere, because they are stopping you becoming a true 80/20 manager.

As long as you trust everyone in your team, and give them every reason to trust you, your leverage will increase exponentially.

People

Have you ever worked in a firm that (in its professional ranks) employs only 'A' people – the best of the best? Most firms, even highly regarded ones, employ at least some 'B' and 'C' people. But when I joined the Boston Consulting Group, I found that *all* the consultants were formidably bright. I didn't measure up to their high standards, but the experience made an indelible impression on me. Working with nothing but 'A' people makes work a constant, fascinating challenge. Many times a day you tell yourself how lucky you are to working with such great colleagues, and you realize that, for this team, the seemingly impossible is eminently attainable. Life becomes a joy.

This explains why firms such as BCG and Apple have been so fabulously successful for so long, despite occasional crises and the rise of competitors that could have wiped them out.

So, who are the 'A' people?

They are the 1 per cent of employees who deliver 99 per cent of the valuable output.

Surround yourself with them. Make sure your team is recognized throughout the firm as exceptional. Hire to raise the overall average in your team, which means hiring people who are more talented than any of your existing staff, *including yourself*. (Very few managers are prepared to do this, yet those who do tend to be both happy and successful. Every hour they are reminded how lucky they are to be working with such first-rate people.) Invest whatever money – and, far more importantly, time, energy and persuasion – is necessary to recruit the very best in your industry. Recruiting the best staff is just as important as attracting the best customers, perhaps even more so. The best customers won't be much help in recruiting the best staff, but the best staff will surely be an enormous asset in attracting the best customers.

The flip-side of establishing a top-class team is that you must move on those managers who are not 'A' players. If they are good, but not quite good enough for your team, see if they can be moved sideways in the firm. If they are not shaping up at all, they are in the wrong job and/or the wrong firm, so help them find the right one. It's not their fault. If you (or your colleagues) recruited them, it's *your* fault. And, however painful it is, you must rectify your mistake immediately. The best firms and teams are always also the most exacting in their standards. You cannot afford to make a single exception. Kindness will kill the team you love.

The 'A' people strategy is the most obvious lever imaginable. If you are prepared to be honest and uncompromising, it is also a very easy lever to operate. It works in every kind of business and industry and in every country on earth. It has never failed. Yet, it is nearly always left in the toolkit because most managers lack the ambition and determination to surround themselves with nothing but the best. By contrast, 80/20 managers understand that investing a little effort in recruiting the right people reaps huge rewards.

Money

Using OPM – other people's money – gives great leverage.

Imagine you are an entrepreneur with a good idea that you think will turn $1000 into $3000, netting you a $2000 profit. Nice. But could you operate on a larger scale? If you make the project ten times bigger, you might turn $10,000 into $30,000. The snag is that you've got only $1000 to invest. But if you can persuade some friends to stump up $9000, and offer to share the profits 50:50 with them, you will make $11,000 instead of $2000 (and your friends will be happy because they will have doubled their money).

Accountants call this leverage, and it's great when it works as well as it does in this example. Sometimes, though, leverage can be fatal for entrepreneurs because it increases their risk and decreases their control.

As a manager with a good idea, you don't have to face these problems. You don't have to pump your friends for investment capital because the money comes from the company. If the project takes off, so will you. If it fails, you won't have to pay back the investment and you will still have your job. So you can afford to think big. Launch the largest projects. This is what 80/20 managers do. It might sound cynical – the company accepts all the risk while you enjoy a large proportion of the rewards – but don't you think your company should invest its money in you rather than in someone who won't make such good use of it?

I saw two examples of this in action when I advised a regional supermarket chain overseas*. The company was the largest in its (relatively small) region, and highly profitable. But it was a family firm, and the many members of that family relied on their dividends to support their lifestyles, so cash could be tight, even for the best projects. Nevertheless, step forward George, a middle-ranking manager working in the bowels of the firm. He noticed that the company had a small franchising division, where, typically, husband-and-wife teams bought the right to the supermarket's brand and were given access to its supplies. By working long hours and offering personal service to

---

* Although the substance of this account is true, names and details have been changed.

their customers, these stores were more profitable than the firm's 'owned' supermarkets.

The franchising division was still a bit of a Cinderella, since it was small and operated only in backwoods rural areas, but George spotted its potential. So when the head of franchising retired, George quietly asked for a transfer to that job. By visiting all the stores and talking to the franchisees (and their rivals), he became convinced that the formula could work in local urban neighbourhoods as well as rural villages. He lobbied for a much larger marketing budget to attract new franchisees, and more cash to train them. Gradually he got his way. When the first three city franchises worked well, he immediately floated a plan for a tenfold increase in the division. The necessary capital was doled out grudgingly, but doled out it was as George's big idea became irrefutable. Within three years, the division was making almost as much money as all of the 'owned' supermarkets combined, and George rightly became a member of the top management team. He also earned a bonus equivalent to five times his salary.

In the same firm, another manager, Carol, was head of hypermarkets. She reckoned this format was the future of retailing, but when she took over the division it had only three hypermarkets to its name. Nevertheless, she was courageous enough to think big. I vividly recall a tumultuous meeting where she presented a plan to open twenty-seven more over the next five years. The projected capital cost was more than the next five years' expected cash flow from the whole group. Of course, Carol forecast a great return on the investment, and she also pointed out the dire implications for the whole company – supermarkets as well as hypermarkets – of allowing the firm's rivals to open more hypermarkets, gain market share and increase their purchasing power.

Nobody argued with her projections, but the amount of cash she requested stunned the whole meeting, especially the chief executive and, even more evidently, the chairman, who was the head of the family. You could imagine him calculating the impact that such a bold move would have on the family's dividends over the next few years; perhaps he was anticipating the flak he would take from his relatives if he approved it. He was squirming in his seat and mopping his brow.

I suggested that the board should approve the plan and fund it by debt, but I was slapped down by the chairman.

It seemed we had reached an impasse, until Carol quietly passed a note to the chairman and asked to be excused. The chairman did not reveal the contents of the note, but after a few minutes he announced, through gritted teeth, that he would support the proposal. It then went through on the nod. Carol never told anyone what she wrote in the note, but the chairman was visibly angry after the meeting. My guess is that Carol staked her whole career on her plan by saying she would resign if it wasn't approved.

There was a happy ending. The hypermarkets were a great success and generated so much profit that the dividend increased annually. Carol eventually became CEO of the whole firm and started to work her magic on the supermarkets by insisting on a major refurbishment programme. She was a master at using OPM to great effect.

Money is the last of the seven great levers for 80/20 managers, and like all the others it is simple and obvious. All of them are available to any manager. Yet few of us exploit any of them fully. Whenever you are stuck in unproductive behaviour, stumped for an elegant way to achieve more with less, you should harness their potency. They are all easy to use, and remember, with enough leverage, anything is possible.

Using the seven levers is a little different from the other nine ways to be an 80/20 manager, in that these levers naturally help and reinforce all of the other approaches. Reflect on this as you read about the fifth way: the liberating manager.

Way Five: The Liberating Manager

You cannot be loyal to an organization and it cannot be loyal to you. All loyalties are ultimately personal loyalties, between one person and another.

Jim Lawrence, Chairman,
Rothschild North America

I don't want any yes-men around me. I want everyone to tell me the truth even if it costs them their job.

Samuel Goldwyn

A liberating manager must be utterly honest with his or her people, supportive and friendly yet very demanding. This has obvious links to some of the levers that are discussed in Way Four – notably caring, confidence, decision-making, trust and surrounding yourself with an 'A'-class team. But there is more to being a liberating manager than understanding how to use techniques and levers. It involves adopting a certain philosophy and cultivating deep personal qualities that are quite unusual, but richly rewarding, in any sphere of life.

The liberating manager brings out the best in all of his or her people for the benefit of each individual and the firm, inspiring each team member to develop and hone their creative side, the small aspects of their personality and abilities that can lead to startling results without the need for excessive effort. Once this is achieved, the whole team will be liberated to operate according to the 80/20 Principle. But liberation requires total honesty and openness from both the manager and the people who are being inspired and liberated. Consequently, it is not for everyone; and it is not even possible in some organizations.

Nevertheless, Alice Marshall* believes that motivating people through liberation is easy. Alice built up a specialist brokerage business in New York and eventually sold it to one of the world's leading banks. She attributes much of her success to a distinctive approach to dealing with people – one that she believes anybody can follow. When I met her, she told me:[1]

> Everything I ever needed to know about leading people
> I learned in kindergarten. Friendship, honesty and trust
> are the root of my approach. People will jump through

---

* Not her real name.

hoops, they will lie down on the train tracks for each other and for me, because they are able to bring their whole lives to work. They can be exactly who they are. Nobody works their best unless you create an environment that creates trust.

Most firms in my industry rule by fear. The culture of fear corrodes companies and people's aspirations; it creates distrust that is never helpful. I try to do the opposite and open up channels of energy within people. When I hire people, I aim to hire friends, to cultivate a lifelong relationship where we support each other. It is a very unusual way of operating. A fear-based culture is all about money – you need a job and health insurance, so people are willing to negate themselves. I've been there myself. After I sold my business to the bank, I continued to work there for six years. I couldn't identify any longer with the company's goals. I felt like a prostitute. If you stay there and don't believe in a company's mission, you lose yourself. That is the greatest tragedy.

You bring your life to work. You should be able to be honest about your family, your children, your parents. If you need to take your mother to the doctor, you should be able to say that is what you are doing. People will call in sick because they don't want to admit that they have a problem in their lives. You get far more out of people if they can be honest. They should be able to go to their daughter's play at ten on a Tuesday morning. I said that's fine as long as you can find someone to cover for you. I don't believe in managing people – that's a phrase from engineering. I give people the latitude to express their imagination. I hold the space that enables people to be creative.

When I hire, I look for people who are receptive and friendly, who are socially fluid. They can be anxious and hungry, but they mustn't be negative. I look for skills and intelligence, but I'm looking at the whole person, for someone who likes diverse cultures and doesn't have a controlling mentality.

Of course, I've made some mistakes, though. There were a few people I hired who were not honest. They claimed to be nice and they weren't. They were hiding their true selves.

I asked Alice what she did when that happened.

She smiled ruefully. 'People can't be changed. They have to leave or you have to fire them. Otherwise they will disrupt the culture of trust.'

Alice clearly cherishes that 'culture of trust', and her twenty-three-year-old son, Robert*, who has worked for a big, traditional corporation for the past two years, agrees with her:

Robert likes his job but the corporate thing is a bit too overwhelming for him. He wants to work in a firm of one to two hundred people where he can learn by assimilation. He's looking for a flat organization, to be able to reach across the table for his learning. His generation wants more personal honesty, to be able to

---

* Not his real name.

go to work in jeans if they want. Quality of life and experience are more important to younger people than money. If Robert makes a third of the pay but works in a start-up and learns from it, he will eventually make the money he needs.

If you were raised to respect people, you can be a good leader. You treat people as friends you'd like to work with for a long time. You say what you think. There's not much more to it.

Making creativity work for you

To get the best out of your people, you need to open up their creative side – the 20 per cent of their abilities and personality that can lead to more than 80 per cent of what they can deliver. That is, you need to liberate them to achieve their full potential, which means identifying their few outstanding personal 'spikes', then encouraging them to nurture and deploy these skills in ways that will benefit the team and the firm. To achieve this, you may need to know them better, in some ways, than they know themselves. And you will need to convince them to jettison – or 'outsource' – everything that they do not do brilliantly.

You will often find that even the smartest and most creative people, especially if they are young and inexperienced, hide their light under the corporate bushel. One of the best publishers I've ever met once admitted to me, 'When I was quite junior, I sometimes wasn't really sure whether I'd had a good idea or not, and often I didn't do anything about it and later regretted it. All I needed was a nudge from someone above me to say, "Yes, it's OK, give it a go, and don't worry if it doesn't work." But I rarely got that nudge, so I remained on a pedestrian career path for several years until I found a boss who told me to step forward with confidence.'

If someone's creative side is to flourish, they need to work in an honest, friendly, open environment. Historically, firms have been extremely bad at providing this; and big firms have typically been the worst of all.

For thousands of years, organizations have been based on power, fear and tight supervision. More recently, the 'Protestant work ethic' has endorsed and reinforced this philosophy. 'Not to oversee workmen', Benjamin Franklin wrote, 'is to leave them your purse open.'[2] When large factories became important, from the 1800s, they naturally followed the repressive supervision that was practised in workshops and mines. Human labour was a commodity; it was bought and sold. The Industrial Revolution herded masses of people together in big factories and big cities, crushing the variability and personal autonomy that had characterized small-scale artisan crafts. Mass production required discipline and standardization. Costs fell as scale and uniformity rose. A handful of inventors and entrepreneurs had to be creative but everyone else had to do what they were told. 'Hands' were needed; brains were not.

Later in the nineteenth century, slavery and economic servitude started, very gradually, to go out of fashion. A few eccentrics – rich philanthropists typically driven by radical Christian convictions, such as the Cadbury, Fry and Hershey families – began to experiment with working communities built on benevolence rather than fear. These non-conformist businesses prospered, but they remained small islands of respect and paternalism in industry's oceans of fear. And even the reformers had no concept that individual workers could contribute anything beyond the conscientious execution of directions from superiors. It was not until the 1930s that the Human Relations School, heavily rooted in academic psychology, began to challenge business ideology and the prevailing management culture.

One landmark in this new philosophy was the publication in 1960 of *The Human Side of Enterprise* by Douglas McGregor, a professor at the MIT Sloan School of Management. He identified two ways of managing, which he dubbed Theory X and Theory Y. Theory X represented the assumptions of traditional, authoritarian, command-and-control management – people would not work unless they were closely monitored, and they were motivated largely by money. By contrast, Theory Y held that people were inherently motivated by curiosity, the instinct to collaborate, and the pleasure they felt from using their own skills and creativity. McGregor did not advocate either theory over the other. His point was that the two sets of assumptions were incompatible and that some managers followed Theory X, while others followed Theory Y. He wanted executives to reflect on their own assumptions and then push their organizations to experiment, to see which approach worked better.

In my less academic and blunter shorthand, Theory X is management by fear and Theory Y is inspiration by love.

Over the next three decades, management scientists conducted many studies to identify which approach achieved better financial results. They reached a clear consensus – Theory X worked well in traditional, predictable, slow-changing industries where competitive advantage was based more on hard resources (the most capital, the biggest factories, the easiest access to mineral wealth, the lowest production costs) than on human creativity. However, in knowledge-based industries, which tend to be more dynamic and less capital intensive – such as fashion, consumer products, information technology, investment banking, entertainment, and the service sector generally – Theory Y won hands down. The traditional approach didn't work at all well in industries where the route to success lay in attracting the best people and encouraging them to use their minds collaboratively and creatively.

Contrast the 'dark Satanic mills' of late eighteenth-century Manchester with the leafy, campus-like grounds of Silicon Valley today. Fear worked well enough in the former. But in the latter, where professionals change jobs every two years on average, and demand for the best talent always outstrips supply, the balance of power – and the culture – is very different. Given a choice, most Silicon Valley executives prefer love to fear.

Logic and most of the research data concur. On the whole, love is a better business strategy than fear, and not just because it is more pleasant. It is more profitable, too. The

Soviet Union lost the Cold War because fear became less effective as the decades rolled on. It works well in an economy of blood and steel; less well in one of jeans and cola; and not at all in one of silicon and services. Good customer service and personalization require love – of the product and service, from the customer and the supplier. Popular music, books, movies and all innovative products, whether high-tech or not, can only flourish in a culture of freedom and love. Such products and services simply could not be made in the Soviet Union and its satellites, but the citizens of Eastern Europe still demanded them. Ultimately, that's what brought the whole communist system to its knees.

So the West encouraged love and won, while the East relied on fear and lost. However, this rosy picture is disturbed by one unfortunate truth. In the Western corporate world, there is still a lot more fear than love. Many bosses continue to manage by Theory X, either because they truly believe in its efficacy or because their firms demand it.

In what we might call the '20 per cent economy' – the really dynamic firms and industries where creativity drives breakthroughs and innovation is the only constant – you might imagine that there is no place for the old methods. Innovation comes from enthusiasm, excitement, intensity, diversity, experimentation and hard thinking from first principles. Surely such attributes only ever thrive in an atmosphere of honesty and personal engagement, where relationships between colleagues are based on mutual support and respect rather than power?

Yet I am struck by how many really successful firms in the 20 per cent economy do not practise benign management. I can think of one in particular where the majority of managers are young and super-smart. This company has transformed its sector through a series of dramatic innovations. But its prevailing culture is like that of a large, old-fashioned corporation. Some of its managers inspire their teams by love, but most rule by fear.

Old habits die hard. It takes considerable effort to cultivate an environment of honesty and creativity – a test of willpower that is comparable with giving up drugs, cigarettes or booze. And just like giving up the poisons we are tempted to consume, liberating our colleagues is entirely in the interests of individuals, firms and wider society alike. It is the only route to the highest levels of collaboration and achievement.

There is nothing soft and squidgy about being a liberating manager. It demands high rather than low standards. A performance culture without liberation is a pity; but a liberating culture without performance is unsustainable. If I had to choose between a liberating corporate culture that tolerates poor performance and an oppressive culture that guarantees high performance, I would pick the latter. Companies have a duty to make the best use of all of their raw materials, including their people. So liberating managers must also be demanding managers. They must insist that their team works hard, not in terms of time or toil, but in imagination and determination to create much better products and processes, to give the customers something they have never seen before, to astound and wrong-foot rival firms, and to become infinitely better and more useful professionals.

Run-of-the-mill is not an option for liberating managers or their teams.

Korea and the limitations of fear

The atmosphere in any office is not just a matter of psychology – the aggregate of the individual characteristics of the employees. It is also a question of sociology – the effect of the culture that hangs in the air, a product of history, the attitudes of founders, the power relationships within the firm, and the characteristic ways managers interact with one another. Corporate culture is elusive – it's hard to define, hard to measure and really hard to change. But it is one of the few vital attributes of a firm that invariably has a massive impact on everyone who works there.

Since it's impossible to conduct a controlled experiment where you change the culture in half a firm while keeping it the same in the other half, no one has ever been able to prove the importance of culture in the business environment. But some interesting parallels can be drawn from twentieth-century politics.

Korea's proud history as a united, independent nation came to an abrupt end when Japan annexed the country in 1910. Then, more than three decades later, when the Japanese were crushed at the end of the Second World War, the

American and Soviet victors agreed to split Korea in half, quite arbitrarily, at the thirty-eighth parallel. People to the south of this line became South Koreans under a capitalist system; those to the north became North Koreans under a communist regime. The two new countries were inhabited by similar people, with the same history and personal attributes, but for the past sixty years they have lived within diametrically opposite political and economic cultures.

South Korea is now a flourishing democracy, with high living standards and the fourth-largest economy in Asia. Meanwhile, North Koreans are impoverished and oppressed by a totalitarian regime built on fear. In the mid-1990s, a series of disastrous policies led to a famine that claimed the lives of at least two million people, with the country's citizens instructed to eat bark, grass and fingernails. The difference between the two Koreas can be entirely attributed to the contrasting ways in which their economies and societies are organized. North Koreans have gradually conformed to a culture of repression, low expectations, low productivity and fawning respect for their allegedly super-human leaders. South Koreans have gradually used more of their own initiative, creativity and skills to start new businesses. Several of these are now world-leaders.

Choosing freedom

As the contrasting fates of the two Koreas show, political and economic cultures are not all equal; and nor are corporate cultures. Where you work, and the culture you inherit and promote, plays a huge role in determining your success or failure. The liberating manager understands this and chooses to work in one of the few firms that encourage high performance *and* personal liberation.

Liberating management is still the road less travelled in the corporate world. The path to full freedom and honesty requires a great deal of wisdom and understanding, and these are still rare commodities in the corporate world. But if you manage to find a company that possesses them, and if you are a decent and confident person yourself, it's certainly a more natural way to work than bending the knee to power. Humans are programmed for collaboration and constructive social encounters. So the effort needed to behave honestly and authentically is modest compared to the return. It is better to liberate than to enslave; and liberation is the only way for teams and individuals to reach the apex of pleasurable achievement.

As a liberating manager, you must appreciate and sharpen your team's few core attributes, special skills, idiosyncratic characteristics and experiences. In turn, this will make *them* great managers and you will be well on your way to spreading the ideal of encouraging different-but-complementary '20 per cent spikes' throughout your organization. Individual liberation can only occur in a culture of liberation. And although that culture may be hard to build, it is equally hard to destroy.

Becoming a liberating manager takes you quite far on a journey of self-exploration, because you must liberate yourself before attempting to liberate others. But the next way will take you even deeper into the core of your identity, because it will explain how to become a better manager through seeking meaning in your work life.

Way Six: The Manager Seeking Meaning

To fulfil a dream . . . to be given a chance
to create, is the meat and potatoes of life.
The money is the gravy.

Bette Davis

I like what is in work – the chance to find
yourself.

Joseph Conrad[1]

When I turned forty, I suffered from great good fortune. After fourteen years as a management consultant, I decided to hang up my calculator. I sold my shares in LEK, the firm I had co-founded six years earlier, and that gave me more than enough to live off for the rest of my life. I had freedom. But to do what?

I had no idea. I decided to stop working so hard and set

up a small investment company. But it had little meaning for me. I tried a spell of not working at all. But that just left me feeling guilty and useless. It was a long time before I realized that I could best achieve a satisfying purpose in life by writing books that, good or bad, nobody else could have written. I am lucky enough to enjoy a relaxed and pleasant lifestyle, with plenty of time for cycling, tennis, walking in beautiful countryside and meeting friends. But I am only really happy if I write something that has meaning for me every day.

Nothing is more important than achieving meaning in your life. Viktor Frankl, the Austrian doctor and philosopher, wrote one of the most important books of the last century, *Man's Search for Meaning*, after he was liberated from Dachau concentration camp. Meaning, he said, derives from achievement – from creating something or performing a deed that derives from your unique imagination and talents. When we crave meaning but cannot find it, we use money, sex, entertainment or even violence as substitutes. We think these will make us happy, but they don't. Indeed, the very search for happiness is misguided because it comes only when we are *not* looking for it – at that moment when we find meaning by losing ourselves in productive self-expression. Happiness is a by-product of leading a life with meaning. 'Only the unfulfilment of potential is meaningless,' said Frankl, 'not life itself.'[2] Bertrand Russell put it slightly differently: 'Anything you're good at contributes to happiness.'[3]

One of modern philosophy's greatest revelations has been

that greatness lies within. Saint Paul talked about the variety of gifts that the early Christians possessed, but as the Canadian philosopher Charles Taylor has brilliantly shown, it was only in the late eighteenth century that the idea of human originality and uniqueness came to the fore. The poet Johann Gottfried Herder (1744–1803), for example, wrote, 'each human being has his own measure, as it were an accord peculiar to him of all his feelings to each other'. The differences between individuals are important, he said, and each of us should tread a unique path and live up to our originality.[4] Nowadays, we take it for granted that we all have a vital inner self, almost in the same way that we have arms and legs, but that notion did not always exist. Indeed, it is profoundly modern.

Despite the ubiquity of the concept these days, however, few people make the most of their potential power within, especially at work. Indeed, there is a widespread belief that managers have no opportunity to do so. Ever since William H. Whyte wrote *The Organization Man* in 1956,[5] managers have been stereotyped as conformist cogs in a corporate machine. Ironically, though, Whyte himself did not share this view, encouraging managers to fight for what they believed to be right, plough their own furrow within the organization, and assert their individuality.[6] Moreover, in the last half century, business people have become much more colourful and varied. Management is now an extremely creative calling with enormous scope for individual interpretation. As Peter Drucker wrote, 'nothing has been disproved faster than the concept of the "organization man", which was generally accepted forty years ago'.[7]

Which other occupation can rival the intellectual challenges of creating unique strategies for each product and service innovation; shaping a firm's culture; liberating and leading employees; interpreting what consumers really want before they know it themselves; negotiating with suppliers, capital providers and customers; and, of course, ensuring reliable delivery of products and services so that the business grows and becomes ever more profitable? What other context is so fluid, fast-changing and unpredictable? What other vocation offers so much scope for unique solutions and effective personalization? What other activity requires such a high degree of collaboration and offers such terrific rewards for originality and personal initiative?

Viewed this way, business requires managers who make the most of what is unique within them. It requires managers who seek meaning in their work.

Meaning is unique to each individual. You cannot borrow someone else's sense of meaning and make it your own. The secret of success on the 'career road less travelled' is to 'do your own thing', but in a disciplined and creative way. Your career becomes a kind of *Pilgrim's Progress* in which you experiment, trying various ways to create something lasting and singular that has the greatest meaning for you. As with the pilgrim, reverses are inevitable; even the Slough of Despond may not be avoided. But these reverses contain priceless information about what others find valuable and about what means most to you.

What does meaning have to do with the 80/20 Principle?

Achievement, and therefore success, in any field goes disproportionately to the few. This is true in the arts, entertainment, academia, politics, sport . . . and business.

The more results depend upon individual imagination, personality and unique skills – the more difficult it is to find adequate substitutes for talented people – the more the Principle operates. When the difference between individuals *really* matters, the benchmark is more like 99/1, rather than 80/20. One good artist may be hard to distinguish from another; but a great artist is totally distinctive. It is the *difference* between that artist's work and that of others that is the signature of genius. For instance, Vincent Van Gogh's later works, such as *The Wheatfield* and *Starry Night*, are instantly recognizable as his because nobody else could have painted them. Pablo Picasso took this a stage further: his work is clearly unique, but he also had recognizable 'periods' when his style became distinct not only from that of all other artists but from his own, earlier work. Great singers, composers and writers all achieve similar distinction. Truly unique artists of all types are the most appreciated, celebrated and remembered people in history because they enrich the world through their difference.

Though this may seem a strange claim, I believe it is exactly the same in business. Nobody else but John Pemberton could have created Coca-Cola; nobody but

Andrew Carnegie could have launched US Steel; nobody but Henry Ford could have founded his eponymous car company; nobody but William Redington Hewlett and Dave Packard could have built their company into the world's leading computer manufacturer; nobody but Bill Gates could have fashioned Microsoft into the software giant it is today; nobody but Steve Jobs could have created – and then recreated – Apple. All of these companies reflect their founders' personalities as much as their knowledge and abilities. The companies themselves and their products are unique, and they have enriched the world through their differences. And this applies not just to famous founders, but to managers at all levels. One particularly talented executive can have hundreds of times more impact than another.

It is good for the economy and society for people to achieve their full potential. It is also the only way for those people to find true meaning in life.

The great majority of economic success goes to a small proportion of firms and managers. The lion's share of success also comes from a small minority of ideas, products, customers, processes and individuals. What is scarce is rewarded. Hard work is not scarce. Long hours, sadly, are commonplace. Loyalty to an organization is neither scarce nor, regrettably, reciprocated. Business school degrees are almost ubiquitous. The tools of analysis – spreadsheets, discounted cash flows, snazzy presentations – are available to all. Even money is not really rare any more. Everything is a commodity.

Everything *except* individual inspiration and innovation.

I don't entirely approve of what I am about to say, but you *could* use the Principle to 'get ahead'. If all you are interested in is self-advancement – the kind that is lauded in what we might call car-crash television programmes, such as *The Apprentice* – then you could spot certain 80/20 phenomena and use them to your advantage. For example, the best opportunities are found disproportionately in a few sectors, a few types of job, a few colleagues and bosses, and a few organizations. Have you ever met a poor investment banker, or a private equity professional that is hard up?

In this respect, your firm (and department) can be much more important than your personal abilities. If the firm is small and growing fast, there will be numerous opportunities for you to engage in new activities, gain experience and discover skills that nobody (including you) knew you had. Fast growth requires experimentation and new ways of doing things, so you learn as you go along. This engenders a mentality of 'all hands to the pump' – demand for talent far exceeds supply. In such an atmosphere personal growth can be exponential. I discovered this when working for Bain and after co-founding LEK – two firms that grew at between 40 and 100 per cent a year during my time with them. I learned more about myself and what I could do in that decade than I did in all the other years of my working life combined. You'll find similar fast-growth firms even in the depths of a recession. They might need a little ferreting out, but it's well worth the effort.

Yet, if you learn a lot by working for someone else's booming company, imagine how much more you will learn by launching your own. Successful spin-offs are more frequent, and more likely to hit gold, in industries where personal knowledge and creativity outweigh capital and organizational muscle. The more capital intensive the industry – mining, heavy engineering and manufacturing, for example – the less promising it is for individual managers. By contrast, consulting, venture capital, investment banking, private equity, advertising, public relations, media, brand creation and management are ideal fields, because they require almost no start-up capital. Information technology and internet businesses are close behind: Silicon Valley and cyberspace are not capital intensive. Tellingly, these are fast-growth industries and magnets for talent – 20 per cent of all industries and sectors that attract 80 per cent of go-getting managers, and provide far more than 80 per cent of rewards to far fewer than 20 per cent of managers.

There is no point joining a firm that's going places unless you learn and contribute to its success. Several acquaintances of mine have become rich without making much of a contribution to anything, simply by being in the right place at the right time. Some of them are the type who go into a revolving door behind you, and emerge in front. But none of them ended up happy; none was good company.

True success rests on unique attainment. It cannot be measured by your bank balance. Unique accomplishments rest on finding meaning in work, and they give back compounded meaning to life. Real achievement makes you feel proud and useful. Sometimes this leads to complacency, but more often it spurs people on to find even greater meaning through even greater results.

Meaning, too – sadly for most people – is subject to the Principle. Very few people find true meaning in their lives, but these are the ones who fuel progress for the world as a whole. Think of someone you recognize as a high achiever in any sphere – entertainment, sport, politics, the arts, public service, the media, business. They will be one of a kind because they will have made a unique impact on the world. They might have created something enduring, such as a song, a technique, a product or a successful firm, or they might have been the first to climb a mountain or explore a new region. In whatever way, they will be a source of inspiration to millions. If they had not lived, the world would be less rich, less interesting, less wonderful. These people find and create meaning in the world.

Wouldn't it be fantastic if there were more of them? Wouldn't it be even better if you were one of them?

Follow the guidelines below and there's a good chance it could happen.

Be incredibly selective

It begins at the beginning. Choosing where to work is as important as what you do while you are there. This one decision – usually made very quickly – can have a bigger impact on your success and happiness than years of toil. I hated working for a large oil company, and if I had stayed there – as I might well have done, given that it was a cushy number – I would have ended up unfulfilled and cynical.

Most managers allow the organization to select them carefully. It should be the other way round. Many managers take the first good job they are offered, and that is especially true when they have been headhunted – it's so flattering, it seems rude to refuse! Understandably, particularly in today's economic climate, many job-seekers go for security, a firm's prestige and an attractive compensation package. But there is always an air of happenstance and passivity whenever a manager stumbles into the clutches of a large corporation.

If you are looking for meaning – and meaning, as we've seen, is essential for happiness and high achievement at work – you must take a different approach. There are five aspects to this.

1. **The field in which you work must turn you on.**
   If you want to be a publisher or a musician, don't take a day job making widgets. If Paul McCartney, John Lennon and George Martin had done that, you never would have heard of the Beatles. Martin became one of the best record producers the world has ever known – he *made* the Beatles by changing their arrangements, most crucially on 26 November 1962, when he told them to speed up 'Please Please Me', which they had previously sung as a slow ballad. Once they revved it up, Martin said, 'Gentlemen, you have

just made your first number-one record.' During his first fifteen years as a producer, Martin had worked for EMI for a pittance (in his best year he earned £2500). But he honed his skills and learned how to spot the bands of the future, including the Beatles. He went on to produce twenty-three number-one hits, and in 1966 his artists were at the top of the charts for a total of thirty-seven weeks – both unbeaten achievements.

2. **The job must give you rare knowledge.** Especially in the early stages of a career, the pursuit of rare knowledge – knowing something useful that few other managers understand – is the route to both success and self-actualization. For example, Bill Gates began to accumulate knowledge about computers when he was at high school, spent much of his time at Harvard using the college's computers, and dropped out to found 'Micro-Soft' in partnership with Paul Allen when he was just twenty years old, judging that the knowledge he needed couldn't be found either in formal education or by working for an existing firm.

More conventionally, I chose to enter the 'strategy consulting' industry when it was only a decade old and joined BCG, the firm that had started and was still the leader in the sector. When I realized that a new firm – Bain & Company – was growing faster than BCG, I jumped ship specifically to learn what was behind the growth. Does your job give you rare knowledge that you can build on and use elsewhere?

3. **The firm must inspire by love rather than rule by fear.** As we saw in Way Five, many firms still rule with a rod of iron. If you can find one of the few that encourages and liberates your creativity, you will soon discover that meaning is much easier to find.

4. **You must like your colleagues and bosses . . . and they must like you.** Establishing a good rapport with your colleagues is crucial if you are to find meaning in your work. And this extends beyond your fellow managers and your immediate boss. You must be in accord with the person at the very top. But how do you get to meet your boss's boss before you accept the job? Simple. You ask to see them during the recruitment process. It's a highly unusual request, but it will certainly get you noticed at the right level. And it will help you decide if this is the right job for you.

5. **The firm must be going places.** Ideally, it should be a star business – the leader in a market or niche that is expanding fast. Only 5 per cent of businesses fit this description, but they account for 95 per cent (or more) of the 'true value' in their industry (as measured, for example, by the cash they generate during the course of their existence, compared to the cash generated by all other firms in the sector). A large company may have dozens or even hundreds of businesses and it may be hard to work out which of them are stars. But you can fall back on an easy test. Are the company's sales growing at more than 10 per cent a year? And is its return on capital employed

(ROCE) more than 20 per cent? Unless the answer is 'yes' to both of these questions, whatever the economy generally is doing, the firm is unlikely to have good star businesses.

Only about one in twenty firms qualify, but don't settle for anything less. *It is so much easier to do well in a business that is expanding and profitable, and has a great market position.* You learn more because you are stretched and you have to fill gaps that wouldn't exist in a slower-growing organization.

If you are looking for work in a not-for-profit organization, you can apply a variation on the star test. Does the organization dominate its sector? Is that sector growing by 10 per cent or more each year? Is the organization's budget growing accordingly? Is the organization expanding its influence and impact? Answer 'yes' to all of these questions and you've found the right organization.

Sticking rigidly to the star test will almost certainly extend your job search. But holding out for a job in one of the few star firms (or organizations) will enable you to find meaning in your work because it will give you the chance to specialize in activities that excite you. A few months spent finding the right job will mean you won't waste the rest of your life.

Own your career

'No matter where you work, you are not an employee. You are in business with one employer – yourself,' says Andy

Grove, the former boss of Intel. 'Nobody owes you a career – you own it as a sole proprietor.'[8] If we take Andy's advice, the Human Resources Department is not in charge of your career; nor is your boss; nor is the company. *You are.* If your career is not how you'd like it to be, there is only one person to blame. And there is only one person who can put it back on track.

Owning your career does not mean planning it minutely, or even at all. Opportunity knocks unexpectedly and sometimes in a muffled, oblique way that is easy to miss. We may overrate some of our talents and be completely unaware of others.

Spontaneity and experimentation are undervalued. A great career is an endless adventure, constantly surprising. Reflect again on George Martin's life. In 1962 he was producing comedy records. Then he met Brian Epstein and gave the Beatles an audition. He had no idea where that would lead, or how it would fulfil some of his own deepest (and deepest-buried) musical talents. He could easily have said, 'Sorry, I do comedy,' and told Epstein to get lost. Happily, he was willing to try something new.

Become unique professionally

If you think of yourself as the sole proprietor of a business – Me Inc. – does that mean the rules of business strategy apply equally to your individual career? Yes, they do. Success comes when you become a dominant star business – enjoying 95 per cent market share of a sector that's growing fast. The idea of competitive advantage applies to managers as well as firms.

As BCG's Richard K. Lockridge said, 'All competitors are specialists. No two competitors can serve the same customers, at exactly the same time, in exactly the same way, at exactly the same cost. The differences between competitors are the measure of their specialization. The greater the differences, the greater the specialization.'[9] The greater the specialization, the greater the chance of extraordinary returns.

It's the same for managers. Every one of them is a specialist. No two managers can do exactly the same work, for the same customers, in exactly the same way. The differences between them are the measure of the specialization. The greater the specialization, the greater the chance of extraordinary achievement. For constructive specialization, your 'product offering' must fall in the sweet spot where (1) you are fulfilling a strong customer need, (2) with unique knowledge and capabilities, (3) that other managers – in this respect, your competitors – don't have. When Bill Gates and Paul Allen started writing software, at the tender ages of twenty and twenty-one, respectively, they already met these three criteria.

Who are your customers? They are your colleagues, especially your boss and other executives. Thinking of your boss as a customer is helpful because, like customers, 'the boss is always right'. So choose your most important single customer – your boss – with great care. A firm might target the wrong customers, and so might you. In other words, you might have the wrong boss. It's impossible to be highly effective – impossible to find meaning in your work – if this is the case. You need a mentoring manager with rare knowledge that you can absorb and develop. So root out your ideal customers – your ideal boss and other colleagues – either in your existing organization or elsewhere, as well as 'real' customers in the marketplace.

How do managers nurture their unique professional attributes? They acquire rare knowledge by working within 80/20 firms. Then they *personalize* that knowledge by applying it in fresh ways that reflect their own mind and personality.

Rare knowledge comes in two flavours. There is specialist industry or sector knowledge, where you learn more and more about less and less. For instance, you might learn how to make the world's most accurate and lowest cost-to-operate speed camera. Alternatively, you can combine techniques and expertise from a variety of different disciplines. For instance, scientists working in the fields of chaos and complexity use insights from physics, chemistry, biology, mathematics and many other disciplines to create models of how the universe works. At a less rarefied level, all management consultants do something similar: they filch insights from academic research and best practice at leading firms in many different industries to create useful models for how to improve performance.

BCG and Bain both had rare knowledge. They knew how to focus firms on their few areas of greatest advantage through analysis of cost structures, competitors and business sectors. They grew fat and fast through studies that produced great results yet required relatively little investigation. The basic insights they utilized had been known to economists and marketing experts for a generation, but they had never previously been combined, and the implications for individual firms had never been thought through and applied systematically to improve results.

Track a few high-flying managers. There will be one common denominator – a spell working in a firm that used knowledge that was unknown to other firms. In BCG and Bain there was an excitement, sometimes bordering on smugness, that we knew things our clients and rivals did not.

Can rare or unique knowledge be transferred? On the face of it, yes. For example, Bill Bain left BCG and founded his equally successful, eponymous firm. Yet, Bain & Company was not a clone of BCG. While using the unique knowledge that BCG had created, Bill instituted a totally new *process* of consulting. He ran his firm in a completely different way from BCG. BCG was anarchic and based on individual brilliance, whereas Bain was centralized and hierarchical, with a few key messages pounded out from the centre and reinforced daily, Soviet-style.

As we saw in Way One, Bill Bain's success rested on his application of the Principle – he wanted fewer client relationships, but deeper and bigger ones. For the first fifteen years of its existence, Bain & Company would work for only one person in each of its client organizations – the chief executive. And it would concentrate all its energy on the few vital issues that would drive the company's success or failure. By insisting on working within these precepts,

Bill Bain cut his firm off from 99 per cent of potential consulting revenue, but he made it both unique and one of the three most successful consultancies in the world. Bain's revenues from each client were ten or sometimes a hundred times the level that leading firms typically accepted. Bill's argument was that if firms enjoyed a high return on the consulting dollars they spent, no arbitrary cap should be imposed on them. And because his firm performed well for its very small number of clients, the relationships lasted for a very long time. Less was more.

I joined Bain when its total staff numbered just a few hundred people – nearly all of them based in America. But they *knew* they were going to conquer the world through the power of the Bain formula. No other consulting firm knew that formula at the time and I doubt that any rival truly understands it today, because it's so alien to standard industry practice.

In 1983, when two colleagues and I resigned to set up LEK, initially we thought we would succeed simply by becoming an alternative supplier of the Bain way, repeating the formula for those clients who had failed to secure Bain's services. That cut little ice, though. LEK only really took off when we applied the insights we had learned at BCG and Bain to an entirely new area – acquisition analysis. Instead of copying what our competitors were doing, we analysed acquisition targets using Bain's techniques and some new ones we developed along the way.

Republican presidential candidate Mitt Romney provides a more spectacular example of taking the insights from a successful firm and applying them in a new context. In the early 1980s, he and two other Bain partners, appreciating their value to clients, wondered whether they might be able to raise a fund, invest the money in companies, and help those companies in precisely the same way as they had when they had been consultants. Instead of a consulting fee, their new business would take a slice of the profits when the company was sold after its performance had been improved. The three colleagues set up Bain Capital LLC in 1984, but with no track record they were unable to raise much money from the usual institutions. After passing round the hat among other Bain partners and their friends, they amassed $37 million – a tiny, almost uneconomic, amount for a fund of this kind. Nevertheless, in its first fourteen years, Bain Capital more than doubled its investors' money every year.[10] It now manages $65 billion and is probably the most successful private equity firm in the world, making far more than even the super-profitable Bain & Company.

Yet money, of course, isn't everything. Furthermore, if you don't believe in what you are doing, doing it for the money becomes a self-destructive habit. I think this is what Ralph Waldo Emerson meant when he said, 'Money often costs too much.' Selectivity, owning your career and the pursuit of rare knowledge are incredibly useful and will lead to worthwhile success, but only if the work intrinsically means a lot to you. So go where the work has meaning, because only by finding meaning will you create something unique and truly valuable.

Before you can decide which job has the most meaning for you, however, you first have to look within.

Finding your core

Successful investigating managers understand the importance of identifying their firm's core (see Way One), and this process is just as important for those managers who are determined to find meaning in their work. They will only work for a company that understands *precisely* what it is and what it does, its reason to exist, and the difference it can make to the world. Such a company knows who its core customers are and understands what it – and it alone – can do for them by making full use of its core resources – the unique capabilities and assets that no other firm possesses. In accordance with the Principle, these companies strip away everything that is irrelevant to their destiny, jettisoning the customers that other firms can serve just as well or better, the employees who don't believe in and reinforce the core, and the capabilities and activities that are nothing special. It is a never-ending odyssey to become more distinctive and useful, a process of trial and error, a quest to define and sharpen whatever is best, most singular and most valued by the core customers – the people who matter most.

A manager seeking meaning must follow a similar path. You need to become conscious of your core personality and skills by identifying the few traits and talents that set you apart and produce the best results, not least in the pleasure you derive from your work.

To derive meaning from your work, you need to polish and hone your core attributes so that they become ever more powerful and appreciated. It's not easy, but answering the following questions will give you some pointers:

- What can I do faster, better, more elegantly and with less trouble than almost anyone else?
- What are the best results I've ever achieved in my life? How did I do it?
- Who are my core customers, the few significant people inside and outside the firm who are most impressed by what I can do and who most value my contribution?
- Do I naturally identify with these core customers and *really* want to serve them? Or is there a different group of potential core customers, or a subset of my existing core customers, with whom I might identify more?
- Am I better at thinking or doing? And what kind of thinking or doing?
- Which few things do I enjoy or intensely experience more than any others? What do I do to 'get in the flow', where time stands still? Why do these few things have such significant meaning for me?
- When have I pointed in a direction different from everyone else and been proved right?

Don't worry if you can't answer some (or even all) of these questions. If you understand them properly, you will see that they are profound enquiries that are meant to promote thought and personal experimentation, not glib answers. The answers might come gradually, perhaps over the course of many years.

If you are uncertain what your core is, experiment with various jobs – even various managerial careers (for example, change industries, or change from production to marketing or another function) – until you find your niche, the unique role that will allow you to reach glorious new heights. But make sure that your core is congruent (or at least overlaps and is compatible) with the core of the business where you work. If it isn't at the moment, move to a firm where it is.

Once you have found meaning, the boundaries between work and play, service and self-expression, humility and success, obligations and freedom, dissolve utterly. Meaning transcends them all, because your life is worthwhile and all of your talents and values are totally engaged. The Principle tells us that a few unique characteristics distinguish you from everyone else. The few things that you have truly mastered and about which you care deeply will enable you to achieve exceptional results.

Fifteen minutes of fame might be ephemeral, but five minutes of meaning is eternal. And talking of time . . . there is another way to play the managerial game which we are about to explore.

Way Seven: The Time-Rich Manager

For tribal man space was the uncontrollable
mystery. For technological man it is time
that occupies the same role.
Marshall McLuhan[1]

What could be more stressful than the daily
battle against time?
Manuel Castells[2]

Michael Eisner, the legendary chief of the Paramount movie
studio and then the Walt Disney Company, once said that
he had taken only one week off in twenty-eight years. He
usually worked seven days a week, too. When his Disney
colleague Frank Wells died, Eisner lauded Wells' work ethic
with these chilling words: 'Sleep was Frank's enemy. He
thought that it kept him from performing flat out one

hundred per cent of the time. There was always one more meeting he wanted to have. Sleep, he thought, kept him from getting things done.'[3]

Frank Wells died in a helicopter crash, rushing from one meeting to another.

Eisner and Wells may be extreme cases of time-anxiety, verging on pathological time-panic. But deep inside all conscientious managers lurks a horror of idleness. It is part of the 'Protestant work ethic' that has supposedly made America and Northern Europe so productive over the last few centuries. If one person cemented the link between wealth and the frugal use of time, it was Benjamin Franklin:

> Dost thou love life, then do not squander time, for that is the stuff life is made of . . . If time be of all things the most precious, wasting time must be the greatest prodigality . . . Lost time is never found again; and what we call time enough always proves little enough . . . Industry [hard work] gives comfort, and plenty, and respect.[4]

But these sentiments, even though they are still buried deep in our psyche, make sense only in the pre-industrial world – the world of the independent agricultural worker or artisan who could rely on his own skill. The game is given away in one of Franklin's quaint couplets:

> He that by the plough would thrive,
> Himself must either hold or drive.[5]

In modern interdependent and complex societies, as we saw in Way Two, the best results require us to collaborate with many other people. We are not self-sufficient; we specialize, and trade our output for other producers' specializations. In this world, slaving away is less useful than having a bright idea and exploiting it. Time-anxiety is unnecessary and self-defeating.

For sure, Eisner was highly successful. When he took over as CEO, he revived the languishing Disney brand by returning the company to its core of animation. Its operating income soared from under $300 million in 1984 to nearly $800 million three years later. Yet an internal analysis showed that nearly all the profit surge came from just three key decisions. Eisner raised theme-park prices; increased the number of Disney hotels; and started to sell videos of the animated classics.[6]

How long did it take him to make those three decisions?

The great majority of Eisner's impact came from a tiny fraction of his time.

Notoriously, Eisner later fell out with Jeffrey Katzenberg, who flounced off to found Dreamworks with Steven Spielberg and David Geffen. Then, after a string of disappointing results, Roy Disney, Walt's nephew, led a coup against Eisner, who was forced to resign in 2005. Were his inability to collaborate and his abrasive, 'micro-managing' style (according to Roy Disney) the consequences of Eisner's punishing work regime? We'll probably never know, but his hyperactivity can't have helped.

Would a time-rich Michael Eisner have been a much

happier *and more effective* person? Probably. And everyone else in the Magic Kingdom would have had a pleasant and more productive time, too.

Does time always mean money?

Consider the following facts, which seem to sit oddly together:

- Medieval French peasants worked for less than three months of the year. According to the historian Graham Robb, 'ninety-nine per cent of activity took place between late spring and early autumn'. In case you are about to hail a time machine, he also says that peasants were so short of food that they spent most of the rest of the year in bed, tightly packed together in order to stay warm and eat less.[7]
- In 1880, harvesting an acre of wheat in North America took twenty man hours. Now it can be done in a few minutes. But though each individual farmer's productivity has increased by more than fiftyfold, Jeremy Rifkin claims that 'today's farmers are busier than ever'.[8]
- Although historians still tussle over what kick-started the Industrial Revolution in the eighteenth century, its technological turning-points – such as the invention and perfection of the steam engine and the spinning jenny – were all due to a few creative individuals: a very thin crust of technologists, managers and

entrepreneurs, including many from deprived backgrounds, who never comprised more than 1 per cent of the population. Without people such as James Watt (developer of the first commercially viable steam engine) and Richard Arkwright (inventor of the water-powered spinning frame and other machines for turning raw cotton into mass-produced yarn), the Industrial Revolution and its economic surge might have been delayed indefinitely.

- The biggest changes in Western occupational structure over the last century have been the continued decline in the number of agricultural workers, the rise in the number of factory workers up to around 1970 and then their steady decline, and the sustained rise in the number of managers, professionals and technicians, who now comprise close to a third of all employees.[9] In addition to there being more managers and entrepreneurs than ever before, these groups – especially those at the top of the scale – have enjoyed a disproportionate increase in their income and wealth.

- A recent survey of hours worked and productivity in the thirty-four member states of the OECD shows that the three countries where people work the longest hours (Greece, Hungary and Poland, in that order) rank almost bottom in terms of productivity (26th, 33rd and 34th, respectively). By contrast, the three countries whose citizens work the fewest hours (the Netherlands, Germany and Norway, in that order) do very well in terms of productivity (ranking 5th, 7th and 2nd, respectively). So, clearly, there is a negative relationship between total hours worked and productivity.[10]

Wealth has exploded over the past three centuries. Leisure, thinking and a good dollop of idleness have been both the causes and the results of unprecedented riches. In the course of the wealth explosion, the link between the expenditure of time and the creation of valuable output has been smashed. Which is more valuable – a lifetime of back-breaking toil in the fields or inventing the combine-harvester? Forty years digging roads or a year dreaming up the silicon chip? The personal computer and the internet are wonders comparable to the pyramids, and a great deal more useful, yet each was attained without the need for countless slave hours.

The value of time, just like everything else, can be explained by the Principle. Less than 20 per cent of total time worked leads to far more than 80 per cent of wealth creation – and not just money-related activities, but those that define a civilized society, such as the extension of education, social insurance and the creation of beautiful objects. A month of Albert Einstein's life created a great deal more than most people are likely to achieve in a lifetime. If this sounds depressing, consider that an hour or a year of your life might achieve something that is hundreds or thousands of times more valuable than anything you have yet created.

Value is not related to time, but to ideas, collaboration and the power of our intent as human beings to do what we do. The further up the value ladder we climb, the more this is true. In creative work – including that of all the best managers – value is hardly related to time at all.

Once we realize this, we become free. We need never again fear that we don't have 'enough time'. Time itself does not create stress. We do, by thinking that our value is constrained by the amount of time we put in.

And yet – and I think you know where this is going – there are paradoxes almost beyond irony in most managers' lives today. In developed societies, management has freed most of us from the worst forms of want, from depending on physical labour to make money, from the crushing yoke of person time (hourly work) as the index of output. We know that small amounts of input can lead to enormous output; and, equally, that huge amounts of toil go largely unrewarded.

Yet, we act as if the opposite were true.

If the Principle applies, some of the things you do must be ten to twenty times more valuable than the rest. Consider a five-day working week. Each day is 20 per cent of the week. Imagine that you do all of your most valuable activities – the 20 per cent that produces 80 per cent of the value – every Monday. By Monday evening, you will have worked for just one-fifth of the week but will have produced four-fifths of the worth. Now imagine that on Tuesday you work only on equally important matters, so, once again, a small amount of your time goes a disproportionately long way.

When you go home that evening you will have achieved 2 × 80 per cent: 160 per cent of your normal weekly output. Surely you would be justified in taking the next three days off, given that you have already achieved 60 per cent more than you do in a normal week!

A few key decisions take almost no time at all but have far more impact than anything else you do. And the more senior you are, the more likely it is that just *one* decision will achieve 99 per cent of your worthwhile results. In these cases, the 80/20 Principle becomes the 99/1 Principle. And yet, standard management practice blinds nearly everybody to this possibility.

The first person to conduct systematic research into what managers actually do, rather than take their word for what they said they do, was Canadian scholar Henry Mintzberg. His doctoral thesis, back in 1973, was titled 'The Manager at Work: Determining His Activities, Roles and Programs by Structured Observation'. It shattered the myth that senior managers thought long and hard about the long-term future of their business.

The picture Mintzberg painted was more impressionistic than still life. The managers he studied rushed around *doing* things, slaves to a never-ending series of crises, catapulted from task to task, subject to continual interruption. He measured the time they spent on each issue and learned that the average was just nine minutes. Quantity of work trumped quality; speed trumped reflection. The managers didn't plan; they muddled through.

Most intriguing of all, they *liked* it this way. They thrived on variety, quick fixes and adrenaline highs. They preferred the concrete to the abstract, the current to the future, emergencies to smooth operations that needed no input from them.[11]

Sound familiar?

Most commentators who deplore managers' lack of thinking time blame organizational demands and constraints. But managers need to look within themselves, because that's where the problem lies.

To operate on 80/20 time, the first priority is to identify the most valuable aspects of your work. Then you need the freedom and self-confidence to focus on those areas and ignore everything else. Most of all, though, you need the temperament and the discipline to think before you act, to resist distractions and to work only on those vital matters that are truly worthwhile.

None of this is easy. It's hard to make your work matter. Your training, experience and habits make it difficult for you to focus solely on the important issues. Taking your time, being calm and deliberative, demands a radical break with the past and with the behaviour of your colleagues. Even if the crisis is really trivial, it's more exciting to address it yourself than to let subordinates man the pumps or wait for everything to sort itself out.

This is why high achievers don't normally work for only two days a week. Why managers find it hard to relax and go home at a decent hour. And why the really important decisions, which require sensitivity to the marketplace, listening to customers' opinions, spotting distant innovators, imagination and the courage to do something different – the occasional decisions that could prove to be turning points in the fortunes of a firm and a manager – rarely get made. There appears to be no time to tackle anything that requires more than nine minutes. So trivial decisions are made at the expense of vital ones.

Yet the truth is that there is *plenty* of time. We just squander it on dealing with exciting 'crises' or attending pointless meetings. We fragment our time instead of consolidating it into large chunks during which we could escape the tyranny of the moment and think calmly about how the future might be radically better than the present.

The business, the firm, is not to blame.

We are. We are not strong-minded enough to save our time and use it where it counts.

But once we accept that reality, the answer to our problems lies in our own hands. We can overcome our time-panic.

As we saw earlier, there are two types of manager. The majority are desperately busy, suffering from the sinking feeling that they are always behind and can rarely, if ever, get ahead of the game. They are harassed, stressed and 'short of time'. They get in early. They go home late.

Then there are the 80/20 managers. This small minority breeze into the office with a smile on their face. They glide through the day and apparently feel no pressure. They are always polite and enthusiastic. They smile. They are satisfied when they go home, which they do at a reasonable hour.

How do they do it?

Saving time by bucking the trend

Alex Johnstone – a forty-year-old manager whose career I have followed for more than two decades and one of the most effective leaders I know – can tell you how. He left school at eighteen and never bothered to gain a degree. At nineteen, he departed the depths of rural Lincolnshire and wound up as a filing clerk and office junior at a small firm I ran at the time. He came to my notice six months later when one of my managers proposed using him on a consulting assignment. By this stage, the consulting industry was well used to employing freshly minted graduates, even from the liberal arts, on consulting assignments. But using an unqualified pimply teenager seemed a step too far. Still, we were short staffed, so I agreed, provided Alex had no direct contact with the client.

It did not work out that way. The camel had his nose in the tent. Alex's research was so good that he was eventually allowed to visit the client (a household name). Before long, he had them eating out of his hand.

In his early twenties, Alex left us after landing a plum job at Goldman Sachs, the global investment bank. He was the first professional there without a degree. Before long, they sent him to New York for six months' intensive training. He is now the head of African Operations for a large American bank, having distinguished himself in the meantime by launching a new product line and making it a huge success.

Alex multiplied the profits of all his business units. But he has never worked long hours. He's never rattled by the 'emergencies' that routinely seem to afflict managers. And he's usually available for lunch – a good test, in my book, of whether a manager truly understands the Principle.

A little while ago, I caught up with him in Cape Town and asked how he does it. This is what he said:

> Look, some things are very important, but not many. I search for tasks that are high impact, which can make a real difference, but can also be done quickly.
>
> I'm responsible for marketing fifteen to twenty different products. For each big client or potential client I work out the three or four products that will fit best – those for which they have a real need. I don't bother about the other products at all, unless someone comes through the door demanding one of them. I approach the clients who should be most interested and keep going until I get a meeting.
>
> I pitch one or two products, having carefully researched why they should want them. Then I listen. If I am wrong, I am wrong. But usually they end up buying one of the products.
>
> They listen because my team has bothered to put themselves in the client's position and understand what they might want. I am very selective in the people I

approach. They have to be big clients or have the potential to become big.

What could be simpler?

'But I know it's not that simple,' I replied. 'Every big firm has a lot of politics and corporate bullshit. It has procedures and strategies and other distractions. How do you avoid wasting your time on all of that?'

Yes, I know what you mean. There is a lot of stuff that can be high time and low impact, required by top management. Right now, I have to write three strategy papers on parts of my business. In my opinion, it's unnecessary. Some managers will make a big deal out of it and spend days or weeks on a presentation and weighty tomes with research and appendices. It should be no more than a phone call from my boss to check we are on the same wavelength on strategy, but it isn't, and I can't refuse to do it.

So I work out how to minimize my time and that of my team on this. I make our reports professional and accurate but I won't let them dominate my week.

I ask what we have done already and look at what we could take from that. Last week I realized there's someone in New York who might be able to help, so I called her up and said, 'Hey, Mary, do you have any research on this?' And she said yes, she did. She sent an email right away and it contained most of what we needed. So all I have to do now is repackage it in the new regulatory framework and combine it with what we have. It will take me an hour, not a week. That way I can have several client meetings this week, and win some new business.

This is *not* the same as time management. You know the idea: prioritize tasks into 'A', 'B' and 'C' and start with the 'A's. The problem is that you end up with a ton of 'A' and 'B' priorities.

It's not time that you need to manage but yourself – give yourself the chance to think calmly and carefully about what you are trying to achieve during your day, your week, your *life*.

'Time managers' allocate tasks to hourly or even ten-minute windows and monitor what happens. This sets them up for a lifetime of failure and frustration. Unexpected events *always* intrude – usually trivial events such as emails, phone calls or the boss dropping by – and they wreak havoc with any carefully drafted schedule. Time management means that you micro-manage your work; it's self-oppression.

Instead, liberate yourself from the small things so that you give yourself a chance of seeing the big picture. Act as if you have all the time in the world – because your best work is so valuable. Be self-directed and confident.

To use time well, you may have to go against the flow. Alex was helped by the fact that he chose not to go to university and landed his first job in a small firm run by rebels. He was a non-conformist, schooled by non-conformists.

At Bain & Company in the early 1980s, nearly everyone

worked their socks off. But Olivier Roux came in at nine and left at five or six. He didn't shoot the breeze at the water cooler; he got straight down to whatever he needed to do each day. Olivier was unusual, almost unique, because Bain hired him from a corporate job – at one of its European clients – rather than from business school or another consultancy. At that time, nine-to-five was not unusual in European corporate jobs. Olivier simply fitted his new work requirements into his old working hours and made it work for him. Initially, inevitably, his timekeeping raised eyebrows. But once it became clear that he was getting through the work, it came to be accepted as a harmless Gallic eccentricity. (There's a lesson here: if you want to keep shorter hours than your colleagues, do so from day one!)

If your aim is to hire people with the potential to become 80/20 managers, I'd go for those who are already used to following a civilized work pattern; those with a more reflective mind, strong on thought as well as action; and those who are natural rebels. You won't find many of these people in the standard corporate world, so I would hire directly from universities (as long as you don't focus on graduates who have studied business, which attracts and reinforces conformity) and from those vibrant sectors of the global economy not yet infected by the long-hours virus.

Less time at work, more effective results

In 2008, researchers Leslie Perlow and Jessica Porter interviewed one thousand professionals – accountants, lawyers, investment bankers, consultants and the like. They found that 94 per cent of them spent more than 50 hours a week at work, and nearly half worked over 65 hours. A further 20–25 hours a week were spent outside the office attending to emails and their BlackBerries. So total working hours averaged 70–90 hours a week.[12]

Perlow and Porter also conducted a controlled experiment at the Boston Consulting Group. On some case teams, consultants were obliged to take one day and one evening off, during which time they were not allowed to use email or voicemail. Meanwhile, other 'control' teams were encouraged to continue beavering away as normal. After five months, the researchers asked the consultants and their clients to rate their experiences. I'm sure you can guess the results. The teams who were forced to take days and evenings off rated higher not just on work–life balance but on job satisfaction, learning, personal development and open communication within the teams. Moreover, their clients reported greater value delivery than the clients of the control groups. Less really is more.

But I think this experiment was tame. When will someone have the courage to test what would happen if a team is forced to take off two days and evenings a week, then three, then four? Let's see what happens when they work just one day and one evening each week.

Eight ways to become time rich

There are eight simple steps to working fewer hours and achieving better results. But before embarking on them, change your attitude. Think of yourself as a revolutionary, one of a select group of people who have made a crucial discovery: that few things in life matter but that those that do matter a great deal. You will achieve great things only if you do it your way, swimming against the tide.

Are you ready to do that? Are you prepared to focus all your energy on the vital few and ignore the trivial many?

If so:

1. **Maximize your freedom to work how you want.**
   Cultivate the same discretion to use your time within the firm how you see fit as you do outside work. Some jobs – even those that are highly responsible and well paid – have limited scope for discretion. An airline pilot or train driver has to follow a prescribed route and conform to detailed safety instructions. A bus conductor or train ticket collector has limited discretion, but more than the drivers – which is one reason why the drivers have shorter life expectancies. The Principle isn't much help to pilots or train drivers. But those of us who do not have to follow a prescribed list of tasks can choose to work only on activities that have a high ratio of results to effort.

   If you are happy doing a job with little freedom to choose how to do it, you're reading the wrong book. But if you like the 80/20 idea, it makes sense to plot your career so that you gain more and more freedom.

A long time ago I worked in what is now stupidly called human resources (for heaven's sake, everyone is a person, not a resource – we are *not* the same as capital or materials or ideas!), and there was a theory doing the rounds called the 'time span of discretion'. It was developed by Elliott Jaques, a Canadian psychologist who was a founder of the path-breaking Tavistock Institute of Human Relations in the UK. (He also coined the phrase 'mid-life crisis', to which the years have been kinder.) According to Jaques, managers should be paid according to the length of time that it takes to know whether their work has been successful. The greater the discretion, the more they should be paid. This was long before chief executives started to be judged by quarterly results.[13]

Jaques's heart was in the right place, but his theory always struck me as a fat-cat's charter – the longer you evaded responsibility, the more loot you creamed off. Yet his theory does embody one golden truth: creating wealth and well-being relies upon discretion.

With more discretion, you can be more relaxed and have more fun. So you should pursue a long, sustained campaign to increase your discretion. Aim to gain a little more each day, each month and each year. Do what your boss demands quickly; then do more useful things. Win the trust of your boss. Make his or her life easier, so that you are seen as a staunch ally.

This may take some time. One of my bosses believed in inputs rather than outputs. He sent me piles of data and articles to read (all of which I thought were entirely irrelevant), with requests to analyse or comment on them. Before long the articles had overflowed from my gridlocked in-tray and were 'filed' all over the floor and on my office shelves. I saw a look of reproach every time my boss looked at the neglected materials he had sent me, increasingly combined with bafflement. Didn't I realize how useful this stuff was?

My response was unwavering. I worked exclusively on what I thought my boss ought to be doing, and presented him with several ideas and projects that made him look good in front of the firm's executive committee. Meanwhile, I began a quiet campaign to work – in practice though not officially – for my boss's boss. I ignored the firm's time-wasting culture and did only what produced worthwhile results. Somehow, I got away with it. And so will you, with a bit of luck and guile.

Spend more time out of the office – at home, visiting contacts, or in a remote location. Don't tell colleagues where you are. Switch off your mobile devices. Discretion increases with distance and inaccessibility.

It also increases with the right job. If an incoming plane is late arriving, if the ground crew fouls up, if the air traffic slot is no longer available, if a sudden snowstorm closes the airport, the pilot is powerless to do anything about it. He won't be able to satisfy his customers and he certainly won't get home on time. All he can do is sit fuming in the cockpit. As one pilot told me, the only time nothing much is likely to go wrong is when he is soaring through the air.

2. **Select just *one* priority each day and tackle it first.** It is impossible to overstate the importance of this. Your effectiveness will increase exponentially if you follow this basic rule.

When you get to work on Monday morning, do *not* read your emails, gossip with your colleagues, attend a meeting, pick up the tasks still on your desk from last Friday, or make phone calls. Sit quietly and ask yourself, 'What is the one thing that I can achieve today that will justify my whole week's work?' If you come up with two tasks of roughly equal value, pick the easier and quicker one.

Then do nothing else until you have completed that task.

It might take five minutes, an hour, or a morning to accomplish. In exceptional circumstances, it might take all day. If it takes longer than that, you have chosen the wrong task. Next time, choose something high impact that you can achieve quickly.

Once the task is accomplished, relax. Chat to colleagues. Take someone out for lunch. Visit a customer or an acquaintance whose advice will help you and your business. Then go home, on time.

On Tuesday, repeat the procedure, but with less urgency. After all, you have already done a week's work the previous day. Spend the whole of either Wednesday or Thursday out of the office. On the other day, deal with unavoidable admin tasks as quickly as possible and then reward yourself by going home early. On Friday, put some preliminary thought into what should be the next week's top task. Then think about long-term projects or priorities for your team and the firm. If you have any time left over, work out the most important thing you could do in an hour or two to help a colleague accomplish one of their key tasks. Then do it.

At no stage compile a 'to-do' list. As you have just one priority each day, you'll be able to remember it easily. In fact, you won't even need to remember it, because you will be doing it, or you will already have done it! If you ever find yourself writing a 'to-do' list, tear it up and go back to the number-one priority.

3. **Think before you act.** Most actions are unnecessary, so you should edit them. Cultivate the art of calculated inactivity. Inoculate yourself against the plague of busyness that has infected your colleagues. Before you start anything, consider whether it is in the 20 per cent of things that are vital or the 80 per cent of things that are not. If it falls into the latter category,

don't do it. An 80/20 manager should not be doing four-fifths of what they used to do. The art of calm thinking and calculated inactivity is so alien to the business world that you will need to make a conscious effort to change your behaviour, but it *is* one of the 20 per cent of things that you must do.

4. **Identify the few causes of success in your firm or team.** Understand the core – the vital customers, resources and actions that matter most to your success (see Way One). What can your team do to move the dial here?

5. **Listen to your core customers.** Engineer a way to talk to the 20 per cent of customers who provide 80 per cent of your profits (again, refer back to Way One). Ask what they want that they are not getting at the moment. Then provide it.

6. **Make your team 80/20 managers.** If the Principle applies, and you keep your people working five days a week, you should see a fourfold increase in their useful work as soon as they become 80/20 managers. But don't be stingy. Give them the freedom and time that you enjoy yourself. Cut them some slack, and continue to help them with occasional mentoring (see Way Three for more details). Their performance will soar.

7. **Identify the 20 per cent of your work that results in 80 per cent of your happiness and effectiveness.** Increase the amount of time you spend on these activities until they account for most of your time. Also identify the 20 per cent of activities that leads to 80 per cent of your *un*happiness and *in*effectiveness – *then cut them out entirely.*

When you are happy and effective at work, time flows. You are not conscious of it passing. When you are unhappy and unproductive, time drags. So eliminate your 'unhappiness islands' – all of the activities at work that make your heart sink – because they cast a shadow over your entire life. (See Way Six for more details.)

8. **Progressively reduce your working hours.** In the 1950s, C. Northcote Parkinson, a British naval historian, came up with a theory that bears his name: 'Work expands', he wrote in *Parkinson's Law*, 'to fill the time available for its completion.'[14]

Working hours are arbitrary. Nine-to-five is conventional today, but it has no basis in either logic or economics; it's purely cultural. During the Industrial Revolution in Britain, factory hours were up to fifteen hours a day – for men, women and children. Lord Ashley campaigned for the Factory Act of 1847, which limited hours for women and children – though not for men – to ten hours a day, six days a week. Mill owners warned that the legislation would lead to disaster. Yet, in Britain today, average real incomes are roughly twenty times higher than they were in 1847. Income per hour is about forty times higher. Productivity soars when time is scarce – when wages are high, innovation is mandatory. The way to riches, for individuals and society alike, is to reduce working hours.

We should conduct some new experiments to see whether shorter hours raise or lower output.

What will the working week be like in fifty years' time? If hours are slashed again, my bet is that leisure and happiness will be higher and unemployment lower.

Set a target for the number of hours you want to work each week. Lop five hours a week off your current level until you reach your target. Working fewer hours will force you to focus you on the essentials.

Ten time traps to avoid

Make more time available – by slashing or eliminating:

1. **Work you know is a waste of time, but have to do anyway.** Almost all managers, including the boss, have to do *some* work they know is pointless. But you should aim to minimize it, and deal with whatever is truly unavoidable quickly.
2. **Working for a bad boss.** Short of poisoning his coffee or hiring a hit man, there's only one solution – leave and find a new boss, either inside or outside the firm. Do it now.

3. **Working in a firm that is going nowhere.** If the company isn't advancing, neither will you.
4. **Working with low-quality colleagues.** Don't associate with people you don't respect.
5. **Long or boring meetings.** Skip them.
6. **Emails.** I love email – it can be efficient and fun, and it doesn't intrude. But most of us overuse it and devote too much time to it. Corral dealing with your emails into two sessions a day – one after you have achieved your singular daily objective, the other an hour or so before you plan to leave the office. Then exit your inbox.

   Never look at emails when you arrive at work, and don't answer work emails when you're at home. Reduce the number of emails you answer and receive. Don't answer unless by doing so you wrap up something important and preclude any further emails on the subject. Don't copy colleagues into your emails unless essential (it rarely is). Don't offer opinions if they won't lead to an immediate decision. (In 99 per cent of cases they won't; they'll just provoke a long thread and waste everyone's time.)

   Don't use email when something is urgent or requires to-and-fro dialogue for a decision. Call instead and make the decision there and then.

   Don't answer unimportant emails. The sender will either call you or, more likely, leave you alone. If you reply to every email, you encourage more and more of them. Make the delete button your friend. Send just 20 per cent of the emails that you sent today; that will give you 80 per cent of the benefit and a lot of free time.

7. **Answering phone calls.** Screen them. Avoid interruptions. If the call is unimportant, ignore it or fire off a very quick email to terminate the discussion.

8. **Anything that is not going to benefit customers in one way or another.** If you can't justify it for your customers, don't do it.

9. **Projects that have overrun.** These are not 80/20 projects or they are being badly run. Either way, get out.

10. **Information.** Most managers spend far too much time gathering and processing information. You don't need to know what the whole firm is doing, the latest gossip, today's share price, or how the market is getting on.

   Bad information drives out good. A wealth of data makes it hard to spot what really matters.

   Increase your access to 'quirky information' – from sources your colleagues neglect or are unaware of (see Way Two for examples). Just like food, a little high-quality information is far better for you than a lot of junk. And it's always best to cook it yourself, from a variety of fresh sources.

Why there is no shortage of time

Parkinson and Pareto imply that time is not scarce.

Have you ever worked on a long project? Was time wasted at the start and in the middle, before productivity finally surged as the deadline loomed? The problem is trivial work, not a lack of time. If 80 per cent of what we do contributes only 20 per cent of our valuable work, we can do without it.

It may sound counter-intuitive, but breakthroughs often arise from leisure and inefficiency. For instance, Alexander Fleming was an untidy man who left his laboratory in a mess when he went on holiday. He returned on 3 September 1928 to find one of his Petri dishes infected by fungus. Intrigued, he grew the mould in a pure culture and created 'mould juice' that he found could kill bacteria. Renamed penicillin, this mould juice has saved millions of lives over the past eight decades. But if Fleming had been a disciplined scientist who never took a holiday or spent much of his time on the trivial task of tidying up his lab, he might never have made his ground-breaking discovery.

There is an elegant beauty to the way humankind progresses. It does so not through slavery or hard work; not by battling against the clock. That's because being calm and at ease is a necessary condition for making the best use of your time.

Becoming time-rich boosts your health and relationships. It's also the way to reach your full potential.

But don't think it'll be easy. In discarding the trivial and focusing on the essential, you will have to reject the habits of a lifetime. Many people who opt for a time revolution also suffer serious withdrawal symptoms – they miss the trivial distractions and don't know what to do with the sudden abundance of spare time. So before trying to become time-rich, you must be really committed to it, really excited by it. You are about to cross the chasm of time plenitude, and you will need determination and mental courage to reach the other side.

The next way is equally effective at generating extraordinary results from ordinary effort. And it probably sounds a whole lot easier to master. But as we are about to discover, simplifying your work can be much trickier than it seems.

Way Eight: The Simplifying Manager

Simplicity is the ultimate sophistication.
Leonardo da Vinci

That's our approach. Very simple . . . The
way we're running the company, the product
design, the advertising, it all comes down to
this: Let's make it simple. Really simple.
Steve Jobs[1]

A decade or so ago, I worked for two years as a manager
in a big company. During that time, I observed a race
between two managers vying for the job of next chief
executive. Jack (a pseudonym) was intelligent and well
connected as he was a member of the founder's family.
Craig (another pseudonym) was less sophisticated – he came
from a modest background and was street smart rather than

well educated in the traditional sense. Both were likeable, hard working and dedicated, but I have a very different mental image of each of them.

I see Jack with a bulging in-tray which he worked through heroically. It usually took him most of the morning. He was conscientious to a fault, diligently answering every letter, email and phone enquiry. He was also a big wheel in the Young Presidents organization and frequently travelled throughout the country and abroad in that capacity. I never saw Craig looking through an in-tray or even consulting a piece of paper or a calendar. He carried his meetings in his head.

Jack ran about half of the organization while Craig ran the other half, and each of them hosted a corporate retreat during my time with the company. I attended both of these (the only person to do so, I think) and found the contrast striking. Jack's retreat was intellectually fascinating, as we explored all the nooks and crannies of the businesses under his control. Craig's was rather dull for the most part, with each of his direct reports simply saying what he or she was going to do, but then he pulled it all together and got everyone excited about their future projects.

I had to advise the executive chairman which of the two men should take over from him. He had his own opinion but wanted an outside view. I had no doubt at all who was better suited, but I couldn't work out *why*. Then one day, as I was driving to work, it dawned on me. Jack was so intelligent and fair-minded that he saw both sides of every issue. He agonized over even the smallest decision and had a genius for making basic issues extremely complicated.

Craig was the opposite. Like a Rottweiler going for the throat, he was totally focused on what he had to do. He could take apparently contradictory pieces of data and reconcile them in an obviously correct answer. His speech was plain and unadorned, sometimes to the point of sounding brutal. *He had a genius for making complex problems simple.*

The story had a doubly happy ending. Craig became the most successful CEO in the firm's history. Moreover, far from being disappointed, Jack was glad to have a good reason to leave the firm. He had joined out of a sense of duty to his family, but his heart had never been in it. After leaving, he carved out a fascinating new career, then eventually returned to the family firm to serve as an excellent non-executive chairman.

The genius of simplicity

In David Brooks's bestseller *The Social Animal*, one of the characters reflects on what the people who had made it to the top of the tree had in common: 'They weren't marked by exceptional genius. They did not have extraordinarily deep knowledge or creative opinions. If there was one trait the best of them possessed, it was a talent for simplification. They had the ability to take a complex situation and capture the heart of the matter in simple terms.'[2]

The best business strategies are always simple, reining the business back to its core customers, deepening relationships with them, and providing only the products that they want.

When Alan Mulally took over as the boss of Ford Motor Company in 2006, he inherited a sprawling empire with far too many marques and models. His predecessors had proudly amassed some of the most prestigious car brands from around the world, including Aston Martin, Jaguar, Land Rover and Volvo. Mulally sold them all. Then he turned his attention to the number of Ford models, which topped a hundred. At the time of writing this was down to thirty and still falling. 'You cannot believe the difference this [simplification] makes,' he says.[3]

I don't find it hard to believe. In fact, I would say Mulally still has a way to go. Firms win when they focus on the simplest 20 per cent – their most authentic and distinctive core, the most powerful fifth of what they are and what they do. The same goes for managers. The simplest, most authentic, distinctive and powerful 20 per cent of what you do should be your exclusive focus. And only *one* thing should really matter to you at any one time.

Star athletes have quieter brains than second-rate athletes because they have the ability to filter out the trivia that usually blocks the mind's vital calculations. Their minds are pre-set so they can perform complex manoeuvres without conscious effort.[4]

But this isn't easy to achieve, which explains why there aren't many star athletes, or indeed many star managers. There are far more managers like Jack than like Craig. Managers love complexity. They instinctively prefer the knotty and tangled to the plain and simple. Senior management is still biased towards those with financial or engineering backgrounds, and the most interesting problems in engineering and mathematics are also the most complex. Managers like uncertainty and keeping their options open. The satirist H.L. Mencken said, 'It is the dull man who is always sure, and the sure man who is always dull.' Contrary to the stereotype, managers are rarely dull.

They will also do almost anything to avoid boredom. And the more intelligent they are, the more susceptible they are to this affliction. This is why they waste their time on trivial tasks. This is why product lines are extended, marginal customers are courted, organizations come to resemble spaghetti, and new projects are always undertaken, regardless of their value and potential. What is new and different has buzz. Fewer than 20 per cent of initiatives lead to 80 per cent of benefits. Yet ever more projects are launched, only to become weeds in the corporate garden.

Abandoning all of this, making work simple, goes against the managerial grain.

M. Scott Peck starts his famous book *The Road Less Traveled* by saying, simply, 'Life is difficult.'[5] He says that problems come when we think life should be easy, and find it isn't. If we expect it to be difficult, we are prepared for challenges and have the ability to overcome them.

It makes a world of difference once you admit that you like complexity. Many grizzled, seen-it-all managers claim to be simple people who like simplicity. It's usually a pose. Few intelligent executives gravitate to simplicity. It takes a genius to do that, and that genius first has to work through extreme complexity. Albert Einstein, for example, used homely analogies of trams and trains to explain his theories of relativity, but he said that fewer than twelve people in the world would be able to understand his theory in its entirety.

Once you admit that you like complexity, simplicity becomes possible and you can start the process of correcting your natural bias towards complexity. Simplicity will still be elusive, though. Compare a manicured garden to a wild forest, or a piece of topiary to a tangled hedgerow. Physicists invented the second law of thermodynamics to express a similar finding – that the degree of disorder in a closed system ('entropy') always increases. As time goes by, everything tends to become more disordered, less simple.

The tag line says, 'Keep it simple, stupid,' but that's misleading. In any big company, as in the world at large, most things are not naturally simple. You have to *make* them simple. It's a constant battle, an uphill struggle. Prune a product line, for example, and watch the weeds of complexity come sprouting back.

'The customer has asked for different packaging.'

'Shouldn't we offer more options?'

'We need a bigger size.'

'I'm going to take this a stage further.'

It all sounds like common sense. The truth is it's common, but rarely sensible. Complexity comes at a cost – always concealed, always sneaky.

Of course, some problems, such as the origins of the universe, or how to abolish war and poverty, are genuinely complex. Sadly there are no simple answers to them. Albert

Einstein said, 'Everything should be made as simple as possible, but not simpler.' Oscar Wilde observed, 'The pure and simple truth is rarely pure and never simple.'[6] H.L. Mencken wrote, 'For every problem there is a solution, which is simple, neat, and wrong.'

For sure, business can face convoluted problems, too; cause and effect often cannot be untangled. The systems thinker Jay Forrester said, 'While most people understand first-order effects, few deal well with second- and third-order effects. Unfortunately, virtually everything interesting in business lies in fourth-order effects and beyond.'[7]

But we shouldn't hold our heads in our hands and despair just because complexity abounds. Not everything can be made simple, but you can concentrate on a few important things where simplicity will set you free. In business strategy, for example, some incredibly useful rules of thumb are *usually* correct.

When you are confounded by complexity, it's always good to recall some insights from the 80/20 Principle:

- Being different leads to higher returns and cash flow.
- A star business – the leader in a high-growth niche – is golden.
- Leading firms should enjoy lower costs and higher prices than followers.
- Most businesses can slash the time they take to deliver a product.
- Most firms are excellent at a small number of things and mediocre at everything else.

- A few customers and products deliver the vast majority of value to the firm.
- Cash is vital and real but profit is an accounting fiction. Focusing on cash rather than profit helps to avoid disaster and builds much greater long-term value. Typically, a few products produce most of a firm's cash flow, while most products drain its cash. It follows that a focus on cash flow will reinforce the need for selectivity and the simplicity that brings.
- Managers are like businesses – they should focus exclusively on the very few things that they do exceptionally well.

While it's true that most problems have elusive causes, that shouldn't stop you from finding solutions. Don't target obviously difficult problems, however intellectually fascinating and challenging they may be. There may be 5 per cent of 'wicked' problems that require 95 per cent of your effort to solve (or, indeed, they may be insoluble). Leave them to the priests and professors. Target the problems that you suspect will have simple solutions. Identify the important issues that can be simplified. If a problem has bothered you for a long time, leave it alone, or give your subconscious the task of solving it while you concentrate on resolving something more feasible (see 'Caring and the power of the subconscious' in Way Four).

Simplicity in action

I once witnessed simplification in a large international firm of specialist brokers. Some of its businesses were going great guns, but the UK business's profits had slumped. A hot-shot MBA was brought in from outside – a very smart and personable manager – but he couldn't solve the problem, so he hired my team as management consultants. We were halfway through our work and still confused when the hot-shot was fired.

The firm sent in a Scottish executive from its headquarters as a trouble-shooter. After a morning talking to colleagues he stunned us with the answer: 'It's profitless growth,' he said. 'You can do the analysis but here's what I think. All the new product lines we've proudly introduced have interfered with what we used to do so profitably. Jettison the new products, get back to basics, and profits will soar. At least, that's my guess.'

His 'guess' proved spot on. In two words – 'profitless growth' – he had simplified the seemingly intractable and told everyone what to do about it.

Steve Jobs was devoted to simplicity. His philosophy was to 'build a simple and inexpensive product for the masses'.[8] The first Apple brochure was headed by the Leonardo da Vinci maxim that appears at the start of this chapter: 'Simplicity is the ultimate sophistication.'[9] Walter Isaacson says that Jobs was convinced his first commercial computer, the Apple II, must have a 'simple and elegant design that would set Apple apart from other machines, with their clunky grey metal cases'.[10]

At the end of 1979, Jobs was inspired by the user-friendly graphical interface that the engineers at Xerox PARC had invented and dubbed a 'desktop'.[11] Today, we take it for granted that we can have many documents and files on our desktop, drag them around the screen, and open them with a simple mouse click. Back then, however, computers were intimidating devices and documents could be found and manipulated only through a series of complex codes, command lines and prompts. The Xerox breakthrough was to invent a graphical user interface that showed several documents on a desktop, represented them with icons, and made it possible for the user to access what they saw on the screen by using a mouse. Jobs and his colleagues were amazed when they saw it. 'THIS . . . IS . . . IT!' Jobs exclaimed, hopping from leg to leg like a demented Indian fakir on hot coals. 'It was like a veil being lifted from my eyes,' he said later. 'I could see what the future of computing was destined to be.'[12]

The Xerox Star, the forerunner of all easy-to-use personal computers, went on sale in 1981, well before Apple's Lisa and Macintosh. It was an extraordinary achievement, but it was not quite simple enough. Moreover, it was far too expensive. Its retail price of $16,595 meant it was out of reach for both hobbyists and ordinary managers. Consequently, only thirty thousand Stars were ever sold.

When he saw the Star, Jobs was hugely relieved: 'We knew they hadn't done it right,' he said, 'and that we could – at a fraction of the price.'[13] The revolutionaries at Xerox hadn't seized the opportunity they had created for themselves. You couldn't drag a file around the screen or drop it into a folder, scroll smoothly through a document, print off exactly what you saw on the screen (the famous WYSIWYG – What You See Is What You Get) or overlap a series of windows. Jobs demanded that Apple's engineers, notably a genius called Bill Atkinson, must achieve all of these elements before they put their computer on the market.

He insisted that computing must be child's play.

He also knew the importance of making it affordable. For example, the Xerox mouse was complex, with three buttons, it wouldn't move around the screen smoothly, and it cost three hundred dollars. Jobs went to an industrial design house and demanded a simple, one-button mouse that moved smoothly, was easy to use, and would cost fifteen dollars. He got it.

Here lies the paradox of simplification. As Xerox discovered, it's hard to make something simple. Yet, if you are not prepared to compromise on simplicity, if it remains your number-one priority, you will find a way to achieve it.

At the heart of simplicity lies accessibility. The point of making something simple is to make it available to everyone, which means making it intelligible *and* affordable.

For example, a group of scientists at Cambridge University have produced a computer and keyboard that will sell for just twenty-five dollars. Yes, *twenty-five* dollars! It's called the Raspberry Pi, it's the size of a credit card, and it plugs into a television. It can be used for word-processing, spreadsheets, gaming and other standard computer applications. The original intention was to make a computer on which millions of children around the world could learn basic programming, but there has also been enormous interest from the governments of developing countries, hospitals and museums.

Simplicity requires a deep understanding of a product's core essence. For example, in designing the iPad tablet, Steve Jobs 'pushed for the purest possible simplicity' and decided that the display screen was the essence of the device. 'So the guiding principle was that everything they did had to defer to the screen. "How do we get out of the way so there aren't a ton of features and buttons that distract from the display?" [Jony] Ive [Apple's head of development] asked. At every step, Jobs pushed to remove and simplify.'[14]

Simplicity is next to beauty, and not far from economics. The way to simplify and to create a mass market is to marry artistry with cost reduction. Jobs did this brilliantly with Apple's laptops and smaller devices, Henry Ford did it for motor cars, George Eastman did it for photography, and Andy Warhol did it for design. Design and art are essential ingredients for simplification and mass markets. After all, what do artists do? They simplify reality while creating something more appealing (or, since about 1900, appalling).

Jobs understood the iron bonds linking simplicity, beauty, artistry, accessibility and cost reduction. He thought of himself as a great artist, and encouraged his team to think likewise. He took them to an exhibition of Louis Tiffany's glass at the Metropolitan Museum in New York to prove that it was possible to mass-produce great art.[15] If you want to simplify products, you need artists and designers as well as engineers, and engineers who think like artists and economists.

How to simplify your work

The essence of simplification is grasping what is and what is not important in a complex picture, then reducing this to something that is recognizable and easily understandable. The Principle states that most things are unimportant. So the challenge is to find the small parts of the picture that are truly crucial and recognizable, and then to render the insight memorably in a concise phrase, or a product in a form that is intuitive and easy to use. A large part of simplification resides in communication – through the product itself, the brand and associated promotion.

The issue must have some emotional resonance; something purely intellectual or rational won't work. A product must have simple aesthetic appeal by being sleek, cute, clever or resembling something beautiful in nature. It is even better if the product boasts technological improvements but looks like its predecessors. That is why, for example, early cars resembled horse-drawn carriages, planes look rather like trains, and laptops have a desktop. It is also why the French, when confronted over four hundred years ago with the potato, called it a *pomme de terre* – an apple of the earth, and therefore a good thing.

Three ways to make simplification easier

1. **Use stories** both to gain an understanding of the idea yourself and to communicate it to potential users. A three-scene narrative is useful. For example: this is where the business started and made its mark (the

past); this is where it is now – overcomplicated and less successful (the present); and this is how to get back to basics and take the firm's core – its few best values, products, customers and/or technology – to its natural destiny (the future).

2. **Use word-pictures** – a few words that conjure up a memorable image in the mind's eye. One cliché that is annoyingly on the money is 'a picture is worth a thousand words'. Just as we love stories, we also love pictures. If someone asks where you were when you heard of 9/11, you almost certainly think in terms of a picture. I can remember the lounge of a hotel on a Greek island, I can remember the decor and the furniture, and I can sure as hell remember the images of the planes crashing into the twin towers. If you use a word-picture, the idea becomes vivid, and the act by which your audience's imagination creates the picture produces a link between you and them. Why do we like cartoons? Because images communicate so much more simply and succinctly than a paragraph like this.

3. **Use one of the stock simplifications provided by the Principle** – for example, businesses are excellent at a small number of activities and mediocre at most of what they do. Try using one of these themes:

   • We've deviated from our core products and customers as well as our core identity. We've unnecessarily embellished our simple formula and

made it hard to see. We have too many new
products and too many new customers, both of
which are different in some slight but vital way
from the old ones.

- We've made the organization too complex.
- Brand extensions have diluted the brand.
  Customers no longer know what we stand for.
- We are suffering from profitless growth. A smaller,
  simpler business would be better.
- Our pricing is too complex. Customers can't
  fathom it out, and some suspect it's unfair. (By the
  way, which big industry has the most complex
  pricing structure? Answer: the airline industry. And
  which industry has invested a fortune only to make
  more losses than profits over the last few decades?
  Answer: the airline industry. Coincidence?)
- Let's back our big winners – the few products,
  services, customers and people that yield most (or
  all) of the cash and true value. Let's make these
  vital parts of our business ten, a hundred, or a
  thousand times bigger.

Reframing reality

Reality is always complex, with masses of data, plots and
sub-plots – and that is *after* someone has tried to impose
order on chaos. Every great story-teller, editor, historian,
politician and analyst manages to simplify the past and the
present. The mark of a great leader is someone who

simplifies in such a way that his or her listeners grasp *one powerful conclusion and then act on it*. Inevitably, simplification always includes an element of distortion; but the distortions of a great leader are geared to *constructive* reinterpretation of reality in such a way that the audience knows how to overcome the roadblocks.

Whoever controls the interpretation of the past also controls the future.

History provides many good examples of simple reframing of complex reality.

For instance, when the American Civil War was about to be won by the North after a bitter and bloody fight, any number of interpretations seemed equally feasible. Was this the industrial North triumphing over the agricultural South, indicating the way the US economy would go over the course of the next century? Was the conflict about the abolition of slavery? Was it about limiting the power of individual states, or about emphasizing the pre-eminence of the Union?

Of course, the Civil War was all these things and more, but would it be remembered as a pointless and brutal conflict, the harbinger, perhaps, of several more civil wars, or as something final and – in some elusive way – ultimately noble and constructive?

On 19 November 1863, two speeches were delivered during the consecration of the National Cemetery at Gettysburg. The 'real' Gettysburg Address was a two-hour oration by the Honourable Edward Everett, an impressive speaker who had been Governor of Massachusetts, Secretary of State, and President of Harvard University. His speech was well received on the day, but thereafter it sank without trace. It was long and not memorable.

After Everett had finished, President Abraham Lincoln spoke for just two minutes. If you're American, you probably know what he said off by heart – and that's the point. 'Four score and seven years ago,' he started, 'our father brought forth on this continent a new nation, conceived in liberty, and dedicated to the proposition that all men are created equal.' He ended, 'We here highly resolve that these dead shall not have died in vain – that this nation, under God, shall have a new birth of freedom – and that government of the people, by the people, for the people, shall not perish from the earth.'

The message was simple – and simplifying. The Civil War was about freedom and democracy. At least, it was now, even if it hadn't been before. You can see how masterful Lincoln was. This horrific battle, he was saying, has its place in the unfolding of American destiny. He started with the birth of democracy and ended with its rebirth, appealing in stark, spare terms to liberal ideals and America's exceptional mission. He didn't even need to state the obvious corollary – that the slaves would be freed.

Simplification is not just about the big issues in our society and our businesses. It is also about *us* – each of us personally. It involves interpreting and reinterpreting our past, drawing conclusions about our future, de-cluttering our daily lives, and realizing that our minds can act effectively on only a few really simple messages. This type of personal simplification is not psychobabble, nor an indulgence – we need to feed our minds simple messages if we are to act super-effectively.

What are your messages? You can work that out for yourself. But I've found it useful to tell myself the following:

- You have a talent for simplification. Use it!
- Simplify the business reality around you. Unite your team in pursuit of a single simple goal.
- Simplify your own life and intentions.
- Life is full of distractions. Life *is* a distraction. The battle goes not to the strong, not even to the most knowledgeable or the most intelligent, but to the most focused, to those who care the most, those who are crystal clear about what they care about, and those who make decisions and act in the face of confusion and uncertainty to realize a small number of simple goals.
- At any one time, have one primary simple goal and focus on it.
- Start the working week with one simple objective. Don't worry about anything else.
- Start each working day with one simple objective. Don't worry about anything else.
- Avoid projects unless they have one simple purpose.
- Design each meeting to make one simple decision. When that decision has been made, end the meeting.
- Boil complex issues down to something simple that everyone can understand.

- Reduce any product or service line by 80 per cent, as Dick and Mac McDonald did in the 1940s, for example, by simplifying the coffee shop and inventing the hamburger restaurant, with no waitresses and few menu items.
- If you are thinking about inventing a new simple product or service, look around for a market that is dominated by complex and clunky offerings. If you think mobile phones suck, invent something better and simpler, as Steve Jobs did. If you think furniture is too expensive, dated and can only be made by expensive craftsmen, invent some that is affordable, at the cutting edge of design and can be self-assembled, as IKEA did. If you think that high-class restaurants are invariably stuffy, pretentious and intimidating, open alternatives that are glitzy, accessible and friendly, as Terence Conran did. The worse a market is served, and the more complex its products are, the better for you.
- Define the core essence of any product or service. Clarify what is it trying to do in one short sentence? What is its single most important benefit to customers? What is its most important feature? Eliminate or minimize everything that is not essential for the core purpose and feature.
- Standardize the manufacture, sourcing and delivery of the product or service. Do it in the simplest and cheapest way possible, which often means outsourcing.

- Develop automatic systems – traffic lights are an early example.
- Eliminate rework. Perform tasks so simply that errors become impossible.
- Whenever you add something, subtract two other components. If someone is added to a project, for example, retire two existing members from the team.
- Ask of every product, every process, everything that you and your colleagues do, 'How can we make it simpler?' If you cannot come up with an answer, you are being unimaginative!
- Make your own thought processes simpler and clearer. Identify an effective, simplifying manager and mimic what he or she does. Avoid what the simple manager avoids. Don't over-analyse. Solve the small part of the problem that gives you most of the solution. Stick to the highways; avoid the byways. Do just one thing at a time – the most important thing.

Organizational simplicity

Simplicity is also important in the way firms organize themselves and how managers relate to their colleagues. Senior managers nearly always overcomplicate the organization by sticking their fingers into too many pies. They insist on frequent and detailed reports from managers down the line, which wastes time and demotivates the troops. They create committees and task forces to search for inter-divisional synergies that may well not exist, and that distract each team from doing what it does best.

Contrast such meddling with Warren Buffett's approach. At Berkshire Hathaway, where Buffett is CEO,

> managers can focus on running their businesses: They are not subjected to meetings at headquarters nor financing worries nor Wall Street harassment. They simply get a letter from me every two years . . . and call me when they wish. And their wishes do differ. There are managers [running Berkshire's businesses] to whom I have not talked in the last year, while there is one with whom I talk almost daily. Our trust is in people rather than process. A 'hire well, manage little' code suits both them and me.[15]

Simplification is the most neglected managerial art, partly because it's so hard to achieve. You will have to battle business culture as well as your own complicating habits. But simplifying satisfies. It takes messy reality and draws the few vital pieces of information and inspiration out of it. It distils reality, in accordance with the Principle, so it becomes manageable, but also so that the vital few facts and goals are vivid and memorable, bringing people together to implement a new solution. It unleashes understanding and shared commitment.

Once you become an effective simplifier, you become a great leader.

*

Although simplification runs counter to the prevailing business culture, most managers are at least able to appreciate the advantages it can bring. The same cannot be said about the next way to become a great leader, primarily because it involves cultivation of a quality that most managers deride.

Way Nine: The Lazy Manager

In order that people may be happy in their
work, these three things are needed:
They must be fit for it;
They must not do too much of it;
And they must have a sense of success in it.

John Ruskin[1]

It's true hard work never killed anyone, but
I figure, why take the chance?

Ronald Reagan[2]

I was shocked to hear David, the chief executive of a large
professional services firm, describe his president, Jacques,
as 'the laziest man alive'.* I soon learned the back story. In
the fight for the two top positions in the firm, David was
supported by barons in the US and the UK, while Jacques

---

* Although the substance of this account is true, names and details
have been changed.

was backed by the Europeans and, crucially, by the profitable and fast-growing Telecoms Division. A compromise was reached whereby the two factions split power.

David was right. Jacques was a charming French manager. He arrived in the office between nine and ten, having walked the eight-minute commute from his swish apartment, which was paid for by the company. After making a few phone calls, usually to Europe, he put his feet up and read the *Wall Street Journal* and the *Financial Times*. Most days he took a leisurely lunch, chaired a meeting or two, replied to a few emails, went for a walk in the park, returned to potter around his large office and chat to the secretaries, called the Telecoms Division, then went home before anyone else in the building. When asked why he got in so late, he once quipped, 'But think how early I go!'

By contrast, David was in the office by eight and left eleven or twelve hours later, often to attend a work-related dinner. His schedule was chock-a-block and he worked his socks off every day. He chaired most of the firm's committees and dealt with any emergencies, of which there seemed to be an endless supply. He also took the lead in marketing the firm's services and making pitches to new clients. No wonder he resented his French colleague next door, especially as Jacques was paid more.

Five months later, Jacques and the head of the Telecoms Division resigned and set up a new firm. This new business soon eclipsed the mother firm, becoming much more profitable and floating on the stock exchange, something the original firm had never been in a position to contemplate.

Jacques continued his charmed life and almost everyone in his new firm lived happily ever after. Meanwhile, David and his colleagues lurched from crisis to crisis.

This saga made me think back to my first job as a newly minted MBA. I worked in an open-plan office and could hear Tom, my boss, behind the divider, as he went about his work. He spent an inordinate amount of time calling his broker and his wife. I didn't need a watch to know when it was five in the evening because Tom left religiously at that time. At the other end of the office, my associate Julian would still be working frantically on his spreadsheets. He was famous for being the first in and the last to leave. Yet Tom went on to become one of the top people in the firm, while Julian was never promoted. I should add that they were equally intelligent and personable.

Then I reflected on my experience in management consulting. I knew two executives who were the greatest I've ever met, in that or any other industry. Yet, in their different ways, they were both self-indulgent and lazy.

The big, lazy boss

If you set up a consulting firm, initially as a one-person concern without any other staff, not even an assistant, you might expect to have to work long hours to win clients and lead the consulting work. But that was not Bruce D. Henderson's way. In 1963 he started the Management and Consulting Division of the Boston Safe Deposit and Trust Company. It was not an overnight success. In its first month, Bruce billed only five hundred dollars. Yet, despite continued lean pickings, he hired consultant Arthur P. Contas – his first full-time appointment – in December 1963. Bruce also used Harvard Business School lecturers as part-time overflow staff, put their names on the doors of empty offices past which he proudly marched prospective clients, and rebranded the firm as the Boston Consulting Group. As soon as he could afford to do so, he stopped doing any consulting work himself.

Nor, mercifully, did he take the lead for long in client prospecting or office management. Instead, he focused on two congenial and highly episodic activities – recruiting and writing. He was the first to hire business school professors and their students as consultants, preferring raw intellect to gnarled industrial experience. But his real passion was writing BCG's *Perspectives* – a series of managerial tracts which, in the early days, were only two pages long and could fit inside a small envelope. Bruce was fascinated by ideas (together with the academics he recruited, he pretty much invented corporate strategy), and he knew that thinking was what he did best, so that was what he decided to do.

Consequently, Bruce's workload was always far lighter than his colleagues'. He exported stress to those colleagues, but did not import it from anywhere. When I joined BCG in 1976, I drove two of his personal assistants to a client conference at a swanky hotel nestling in a beautiful forest so that they could prepare for the arrival of the founder. I remember Bruce as a big man in every sense of the word – formidable, detached, interrogative and intimidating. He didn't ask me a word about my clients or my work, but quizzed me relentlessly about some obscure business theory. When it was clear I couldn't answer his questions, he delivered a forty-five-minute lecture that I'm sure would have been fascinating if I hadn't been scared stiff.

Bruce minimized the time he spent on work he didn't want to do. He awarded himself a life I can only envy – handing down oracular pronouncements, stimulating new ideas among super-intelligent colleagues, and touring the world in style to visit his many offices. Yet, by doing only what he wanted to do, spending all of his time on what he did best, he drafted a blueprint for a vastly better use of resources in business. On the other hand, he relied on an army of highly paid but highly stressed consultants, typically working between sixty and ninety hours a week (and billing by the hour). I was one of those high-wage slaves and it wasn't pretty.

William Worthington Bain, Jr. – Bill Bain or 'Mr Big' to *his* overpaid and overworked serfs – is another wonderful illustration of economy in action. Bill majored in history at Vanderbilt University, graduated in 1959, tried a couple of jobs that didn't work out, then returned to Vanderbilt the following year as a fundraiser. In that capacity he approached Bruce Henderson, another Vanderbilt alumnus, for funds to help start the university's business school. Despite Bill's obvious lack of business qualifications, Bruce subsequently offered him a job at BCG. There is a story that Bruce spent an airline flight teaching Bill the principles of depreciation, but before long the new recruit was heading one of the four teams that Bruce had created to stimulate internal competition. Bill's team demonstrated the greatest growth in revenues. A clear vindication of Bruce's good judgement in hiring and fast-tracking Bill? Yes and no. Bill wanted to run his own firm and in 1973 he resigned and took several of his BCG team with him to found Bain & Company. Bruce took their defection badly. He told the *New York Times*, 'it was war – the Japanese bombing of Pearl Harbor. I felt more betrayed and robbed and desecrated than ever before.'[3]

I was not a very successful consultant at BCG and left to join Bain in 1980. I was startled when I was soon made a partner (as was everyone else!). Partners from around the world had to travel to Boston once a month for a meeting, which Bill ruled with consummate authority, although he never raised his voice. He was one of the most impressive and singular people I've ever met, and he managed to create an amazingly powerful and lucrative firm with the minimum of personal effort. Like Bruce Henderson, he rapidly withdrew from all client work. On those occasions when he turned up, he cocooned himself in his huge and beautifully appointed office, replete with antiques and basketball memorabilia, an oasis of calm and culture away from the hubbub of the cramped, open-plan main office. His secretary kept all-comers at bay – 'there are so many artificial constraints in Bill's diary', a senior partner told me once. I encountered him just once in the lift. He was impeccably dressed in full tennis regalia.

Bill led a charmed life. Underneath him was a sharply

defined pyramid. There were five of his original colleagues – including John Halpern and Ralph Willard – whom I grew to admire enormously for their skill in selling ever more of our services to the same clients. (Though it has to be said that perhaps John lacked subtlety. I remember him commending our work to the client board with the words, 'This strategy will make everyone in this room rich.') These five lieutenants talked to Bill, and Bill talked to them, much as God speaks to His angels but rarely to anyone else. Beneath the angels came the ordinary partners. Beneath us, there were the project managers. Then came the consultants. And finally, a Bain innovation, there were the research associates – ordinary graduates without a business degree. Everyone – from the famous five downward – worked all the hours Bill demanded and faithfully executed everything asked of them by the next level up.

Bill was said to retain most of the profits. I don't know precisely how much these were, since mere partners were never allowed to see the firm's books (even though we all had unlimited liability). As one of the longer-standing partners once whispered to me, the partnership agreement was not a Bill of Rights, but rather the rights of Bill! His hourly rate must have been extraordinary.

I do not complain, though. Bill had a vision of a consulting firm in an intimate relationship with a relatively small number of big client firms. In his view, a consulting engagement was like a marriage – a long-term partnership of equals for mutual benefit. The senior Bain partner would develop an intimate rapport with the client's chief executive, such that the latter would *never* make an important decision without first asking Bain & Company's advice. The CEO would also agree not to impose any cap on Bain's billings, provided their company earned a return of five to ten times annual profits on any consulting expenditure. In the early 1980s, McKinsey, the consulting industry leader, would rarely charge a single client more than two million dollars a year. Bain & Company was reputed to charge some of its clients ten times that, if not more. For any client organization, Bain started by exhaustively devising a strategy for the whole firm – every division, every country. This usually took a few years. We then moved on to cost reduction and other forms of 'implementation' of the strategy. When this showed signs of flagging, we would work on an acquisition for the client and the cycle would start anew. Then there would be more acquisitions. As long as the client firm prospered and the CEO stayed in place, so did Bain, and our revenues grew ever higher.

It probably didn't take Bill Bain long to work out this ingenious formula and then to build his firm around it. But the value created for Bain & Company – and usually for the client, too – was astronomical. Bill spent his time on what he was uniquely qualified to do. His output bore no relation to the time or effort he inputted. But if Bill had been more activist, I doubt that he ever would have dreamed up this amazing wealth-creation system. Also, I believe his lack of an MBA helped enormously. If Bill had been fascinated by the nuts and bolts of consulting, as 99.9 per cent of consultants are, he probably would not have had the vision of a totally different way of doing it.

Surely it is significant that the two most creative and influential management consultants of the last sixty years – a pair of business leaders who founded two of the three most prestigious consulting firms in the world today – were arguably the idlest, too.

The right sort of laziness

There is an old joke about a wealthy young Englishman on a grand tour of Europe before the First World War. He stumbles across twelve young beggars in Naples, lying in the shade, doing nothing at all. 'Who is the laziest of you all?' the visitor asks. 'I'll give you a coin.' Eleven of the boys jump up, clamouring for his lira. But he gives it to the twelfth vagrant, who hasn't moved a muscle.

This story was told by Bertrand Russell, the great mathematician and philosopher, in his essay 'In Praise of Idleness'. He wrote,

> Work is of two kinds: first, altering the position of matter at or near the earth's surface relatively to other such matter; second, telling other people to do so. The first is unpleasant and ill paid; the second is pleasant and highly paid. The second kind is capable of indefinite extension: there are not only those who give orders, but those who give advice as to what orders should be given.
>
> I think there is far too much work done in the world,

that immense harm is caused by the belief that work is virtuous . . . The road to happiness and prosperity lies in an organized diminution of work.[4]

The Prussian aristocrat General Field Marshall Erich von Manstein came to hold similar views, although he arrived at them via a completely different route. Manstein was a successful professional soldier who despised Hitler yet was one of his greatest assets. He directed the stunning *Blitzkrieg* that quickly brought France to its knees in 1940 and then took charge of the German XIth Army that had similar success against the Russians in the Crimea, capturing Sevastopol with great ingenuity in July 1942. In 1943–4, he wavered when asked to join the plot against Hitler, at first agreeing to participate and then distancing himself from the conspirators. He was imprisoned by the British for war crimes in 1948 but released in 1953. Thereafter, he lived a quiet life until his death in Munich, aged eighty-five, though his memoir became a best-seller in post-war Germany.[5]

Manstein divided the officers under his command into four types, according to whether they were stupid or intelligent, and hard-working or lazy. Then he gave great advice for how to deal with each type:

1. Lazy, stupid officers: 'leave them alone – they do no harm'.
2. Hard-working, intelligent officers: 'they make excellent staff officers, ensuring that every detail is

properly considered'.

3. Hard-working, stupid officers: 'they are a menace and create irrelevant work for everyone. They must be fired at once.'

4. Lazy, intelligent officers: 'they are suited to the highest office'.

The same principles can be applied to managers:

Manstein reminds us that laziness itself is not a virtue. It works well only when it is complemented by high intelligence. Moreover, the very highest-achieving managers I've observed also possess a host of other virtues – such as thoughtfulness, originality and vision – as well as some less attractive qualities, including at least a pinch of arrogance, narcissism and self-indulgence. They place a very high value on their own time and having the freedom to think things through without being disturbed, and therefore on their comfort and desire to avoid the tedious chores that the rest of us often tackle keenly to demonstrate our democratic credentials.

These super-performers are undoubtedly lazy, but theirs is an unusual kind of laziness, closely related to creativity. Their brilliance gives them the confidence to be lazy, and their laziness gives them the freedom (from the normal pressures of work) to find shortcuts to better results through less effort. Jacques, Bruce and Bill would not have been so lazy if they had not been so imaginative; and they would not have been so imaginative if they had worked harder. The strongest link, though, is between laziness and self-indulgence, on the one hand, and a kind of inspired determination, on the other. We do not normally associate laziness with determination, but the determination to find a much better solution involving much less effort is the highest form of laziness. It is the very essence of the 80/20 Principle in action. Those who practise it are *visionary* managers – lazy, thoughtful, inventive and possessing a self-confidence bordering on the most constructive form of arrogance.

Laziness and selectivity also go hand in hand. The lazy manager has to be selective; and the selective manager can afford to be lazy. Selectivity and success are closely related, too. Once you understand that very few actions and decisions will have a disproportionately huge impact on your career or the fortunes of your company, you naturally search for those very few big breaks. You don't sweat about the small stuff, because small drives out big. Warren Buffett – the world's most successful investor, with a net worth of around fifty billion dollars – says that the great majority of his fortune has resulted from fewer than ten crucial decisions. At the time of writing, Buffett was eighty-two, and he has been making money since he was a small child, so that is just a fraction more than one important decision a decade. It is easier to make a few really good decisions if you don't waste your time on things that will never be life-changing. Laziness, selectivity and confidence compound each other and are the nearest we can get to a short formula for extraordinary achievement.

How to make yourself lazy

Before we leave Way Nine, though, what about those of us who are not naturally lazy or unusually selfish? Not all super-performers are naturally lazy. For instance, Bertrand Russell achieved a huge amount in his long life. Although he praised idleness in others, he admitted that he himself was not idle. 'I believed all I was told [about the virtues of hard work],' he wrote, 'and acquired a conscience that has kept me working hard down to the present moment.'[6]

It is probably the same for you – most managers are hard-working. I myself have tried hard to become more lazy throughout my life . . . but it's been a struggle! Having worked up to ninety hours a week during my time at Bain, I cut this down to forty or fifty hours when I co-founded LEK. However, I concealed my 'laziness' from my colleagues by being out of the office a lot and working unusual hours, often taking a long break in the middle of the day for exercise or meeting friends, and returning to work late in the evening.

When I hit forty, I cut my hours down again. Now I work no more than three hours a day, unless you count pleasurable reading and talking as work – which in a way it is for me, because that's when I have my best ideas. If I am lucky enough to be inspired, it usually comes when I am cycling, walking, on holiday, or sleeping. I know that I achieve more when I work less. Yet, when I am idle, I still find it hard not to feel at least a little guilty.

Christopher Morley extolled

> philosophical laziness . . . the kind of laziness that is based upon a carefully reasoned analysis of experience. Acquired laziness. We have no respect for those who were born lazy. It is like being born a millionaire – they cannot appreciate their bliss. It is the man who has hammered his laziness out of the stubborn material of life for whom we chant praise.[7]

As John W. Raper said, 'There is no pleasure in having nothing to do. The fun is having lots to do and not doing it.'[8]

Laziness really does work, even if you are not fortunate enough to be naturally lazy. Of course, you cannot be lazy in every kind of job. You need to find one where you control your own hours and are unsupervised – which is one reason why so many lazy achievers start their own enterprises. Furthermore, laziness is not easy to achieve – sometimes you will master it only towards the end of your career, and you will certainly need determination to stick with it along the way. Ultimately, though, it's worth it, because lazy managers achieve exceptional results.

Only by being economical with your energy and attention can you make it count when it matters.

If practising lazy management is difficult, the final way to become an 80/20 manager can be even more demanding. It is, however, often also the most valuable and rewarding route. This is the world of the strategic manager.

Way Ten: The Strategic Manager

> The future belongs to those who believe in
> the beauty of their dreams.
>
> Eleanor Roosevelt

Strategic managers create fantastic value by re-imagining their industry. By devising fresh ways of doing business, they provide unique products or services for which customers are happy to pay a premium, or they cut costs without reducing quality, or, ideally, they do both – they sell for more and produce for less. The new way of doing business is highly profitable – it is an 80/20 solution.

It is not easy to become a strategic manager, but the benefits can be astronomical – to the manager, to the customers and to the company's workers.

The pioneers of strategic management

At the age of thirty, my career was stalling badly. I'd failed to gain promotion despite four years of hard slog at the

Boston Consulting Group. My response was to ratchet up the hours and effort even further, until I was working at least ten-hour days, seven days a week. I stopped exercising, got a bit tubby, and neglected my personal life. But trying harder didn't work.

Utterly miserable, I resigned before I was fired, spent a month driving my Porsche – soon to be repossessed – around the south of France, went for long walks, and took even longer lunches and dinners. I also looked for other jobs.

I ended up in Zurich one sunny afternoon, talking to a charming Swiss gentleman called Egon Zehnder. He had founded his eponymous firm in 1964, and over the next sixteen years had turned it into one of the world's top headhunting companies. Friendly, immaculately dressed, and with a deep voice, he made a profound impression on me. He was a strategic manager, because his idea of a headhunting firm was totally different from those of his American competitors.

I can still recall him explaining the three main differences. First, he recruited only people of outstanding intellect, so his staff were always able to keep up with even the smartest clients. Previously, nobody in his industry had believed that a first-class degree was necessary or even particularly desirable. Second, he hired only warm and collaborative people, and he set the firm's incentives so that trust, loyalty and team spirit would flourish. In 1976, he had given up his majority ownership of the company – even then, it had been worth tens of millions of dollars

– and handed each partner an equal equity stake and share of profits. To ensure all of the offices helped one another, there was a single global profit pool. To encourage colleagues to take a long-term view, compensation was linked to seniority. Third, he broke with the industry standard of taking a percentage of the newly placed executive's salary from the client. Instead, he charged a fixed fee, thereby ensuring that his firm's interests always mirrored those of the client.

Egon Zehnder was a strategic manager because he thought long and hard about how to achieve extraordinary results – for his clients and his firm – while employing professionals who cost no more than those in rival firms. He came up with a superior business model for his industry. As we've seen in earlier chapters, Bill Bain was doing something similar in the consulting industry around the same time. He was in the process of pioneering a radically new system based on working intensively for only one client in a particular sector and transforming their performance as a result. Having decided that headhunting wasn't for me, I soon joined Bain and gained first-hand experience of Bill's formula in practice. It was undoubtedly a wonderful system.

Labelling someone a strategic manager reveals absolutely nothing about their philosophy, management style or skill in managing people. Although he graduated from Harvard Business School, Egon was a European to his fingertips: he believed in a collegiate, congenial, long-term partnership of equals, not in hierarchy or maximizing his firm's profits.

Bruce Henderson and Bill Bain, by contrast, were both red-blooded capitalists. But there the similarity between them ends. Bruce was challenging, difficult to deal with, and an individualist to his core. He wanted intelligent people to think for themselves and create new intellectual insights. I have never met anyone who believed so strongly in freedom and spontaneity. Bill was the complete opposite: he told people what to do and expected them to follow his instructions to the letter. Much smoother than Bruce, and not in the least impetuous, he worked out his central insights and then put them into practice through a perfect system of command and control that left nothing to chance.

The struggle for supremacy between Bill and Bruce can be viewed as a microcosm of the achievements and contradictions of the American system – the ceaseless conflict between libertarian creativity, on the one hand, and ruthless organizing genius imposing a better way, on the other. It echoes the splintering of religion into thousands of churches and sects versus the 'city on the hill' idea that there is only one true way. It is Silicon Valley versus the US Army, the internet versus the FBI, Apple versus Microsoft. Yet Bruce and Bill, Silicon Valley and the US Army, the internet and the FBI, Apple and Microsoft, like everything else in America, were and are all moulded by great individuals who were and are given unusual and sometimes dangerous licence to do their own thing. To a degree not true anywhere else in the world, achievement in America is personal, based on idiosyncratic insights and the freedom and inclination to put them to work by creating new organizations or reinventing old ones.

Given the sometimes profound differences in style and ideology, what do all strategic managers have in common? Each of them has a unique insight into his or her industry, a radical vision for a better way of doing business within it, and uncompromising determination to bring it about. For example:

- Herb Kelleher came up with a new model for an airline that is low cost, fun and highly profitable. Southwest now carries more passengers within the United States than any other airline.
- Bruce Henderson had the insight that a 'thinking firm' – employing the brightest young people who are interested in understanding how business works – could become a world leader in the management consulting industry.
- Bill Bain had the insight that a consulting firm could form a very tight and intimate relationship with a client organization and especially the CEO.
- Egon Zehnder reckoned he could transform the headhunting industry by hiring only highly intelligent, warm and approachable people and encouraging them to collaborate with the firm's other offices by instituting a single global profit pool.
- Mark Zuckerberg took the real-world college

'facebook', in which students shared their interests and pictures, and translated it into cyberspace to create a radically new kind of social networking site.

- Andrew Black and Edward Wray founded Betfair and turned the betting industry on its head, by allowing gamblers to bet against each other for a very low fee.

- In 1996, Larry Page and Sergey Brin had the vision 'to organize the world's information and make it universally accessible'.[1] To do this, their firm, Google, developed a superior type of search engine, far faster and simpler than that of the search pioneers, ventures that are now forgotten. Google now processes over a billion search requests every day. Google demonstrates that strategic managers do not have to invent the industry they may come to dominate. But if you are not first, you have to do things completely differently and dramatically better.

- In South Africa, Raymond Ackerman's supermarkets were different. Pick and Pay's role, he said, was to work for consumers rather than for suppliers or the firm itself. This idea was anything but anodyne. It involved taking on powerful vested interests, as when Raymond sold cut-price petrol in contravention of a shady deal brokered between the apartheid government and the big oil companies. Yet, as Ackerman constantly told me, 'doing good is good business.' In the 1970s and 1980s his chain expanded rapidly and became unusually profitable.

The essential characteristics of the strategic manager

Strategic managers often reach for the stars, but strategic management can be applied to any level of ambition – as long as it yields exceptional results for unexceptional effort. You can find strategic managers in all types of business, and indeed outside it. For instance, when I was at grammar school in England, one of my masters was an eccentric named W.G. Babbington. His innovation was to teach from a comfortable chair raised on a dais at the front of the class. Seated next to him was his 'right-hand man', a position held in rotation by each class member. The right-hand man would conduct most of the lesson, select questions from the other pupils, and, if possible, answer them himself or find others who could. For the first and last five minutes of each class, we listened to Mr Babbington's favourite classical records. The system he devised made work easy and enjoyable for him, and it gave us a terrific learning experience.

All strategic managers value thought above action. Unlike most of their colleagues, they never let action – or conformity – drive out thought. Then they think very hard about how to do more with less. This isn't easy, though, which explains why good strategic thinking is rare in the business world. Following a routine, meeting colleagues, calling or emailing and visiting customers all come much more naturally to most managers. So it takes a lot of determination to reject all of them and devote most of your time to thinking. At first, this will feel uncomfortable because you will be engaging in something novel. It's like walking several miles after you've spent the last few years driving everywhere. But our bodies are designed to walk, and our brains are designed to think, so if you persevere both become almost effortless.

Mastering the art of thinking is only the first step to becoming a strategic manager, though, because serious thought inevitably leads to uncertainty: after all, if there wasn't uncertainty, there would be no need to think. Thinking always involves risk – it may force you to commit to something unfamiliar, daunting and possibly even harmful. Acting on an innovative idea is a gamble because you will be staking your reputation, time, energy and the firm's resources without knowing what will happen. But bear in mind that everything that has made the modern world what it is today – from mechanized agriculture, the Industrial Revolution and refrigeration to modern medicine, cyberspace and all of those mobile devices that have remodelled our daily routines – has come from a gamble based on hard thought. Every new project or management initiative begins with a single thought, a hypothesis, a guess or a conviction that we have the capacity to achieve more with less.

Successful strategic managers also need the extreme ambition to create a better business model, an understanding of how to achieve this, and, finally, the determination to make it happen. Once those elements are all in place, though, the rewards for one bright idea can be enormous.

Of course, many innovators have had what they thought were ingenious ideas, but we've never heard of them because they failed. In all probability, their new business models weren't *dramatically* better than existing ones. New empires are founded on revolutions, not on slight improvements. Equally, if an idea is genuinely innovative but does not lead to higher prices or lower costs for the company, it will fail. And, finally, many great ideas fall by the wayside because the people who think them up do not have the necessary ambition, practical skill, courage or obsessive drive to make them succeed. The faint-hearted do not become successful strategic managers.

The secrets of strategic success

There are, then, plenty of reasons why your idea might fail, no matter how revolutionary it is. But if you have a hunch as to how your industry could be reconstructed, if you know what it lacks that a totally different approach might bring, and if you have an inkling of what that approach might be, you should pursue it . . . because you might be well on your way to founding the next Google or Facebook.

Reviewing the strategic managers I've known over the years, and observing what they did, reveals certain clues as to how they became great successes in their respective fields:

- Often, the most fundamental difference is a new type of person brought into the industry, and/or a new way of organizing them to encourage a very high degree of collaboration throughout the new firm.

- One common theme is taking the very smartest and most motivated people and providing them with a template of how to behave. Although the template is very specific, it is also liberating. As long as you follow the *values* of the founder, you are given great latitude to utilize your personal assets however you see fit to achieve results. Authenticity is not enough; nor is discipline. But disciplined authenticity triumphs time and again.

- The economics work – costs are lower and margins are fatter (sometimes despite lower prices) than in the traditional model.

- The appeal to customers is different. BCG was the first consulting firm to appeal primarily to its clients' intellects, and the first to hire and promote based on raw intellect. No consultant prior to Bill Bain had focused on the personal interests and ambitions of the chief executive. Nobody before Herb Kelleher had tried to make flying low-cost, yet also fun for passengers *and* staff. Mark Zuckerberg was the first entrepreneur to realize that students were a huge, largely untapped market for online social networking. Nobody before Larry Page and Sergey Brin had integrated advertisers so seamlessly into search algorithms. Nobody before Andrew Black and Edward Wray had targeted large-scale gamblers who were capable of making regular profits on their betting.

- There is often a strong emotional link between the founder, the managers in the new firm and the customers. Sometimes the founder becomes a figurehead: he or she personifies the firm's values and provides extraordinary (as well as very cheap and highly effective) publicity. Think of what Richard Branson's high profile has done for Virgin. The founder stands for something. The founder *is* the brand. The founder may also be the model for the organization.

Given these hints, how would you transform your industry?

The strategic manager – the ultimate 80/20 manager

The paradox of the strategic manager is that it is easy to *be* one – work and life flow almost effortlessly down a lush stream – but it is extraordinarily difficult to *become* one. Some people manage it only after accumulating decades of experience in their chosen career. Nevertheless, of the ten ways to become an 80/20 manager, the strategic manager is the most quintessentially '80/20'. So much is gained, including a huge dollop of fun, for relatively little effort, because the original idea is so good.

Does that turn you on? If so, you can scale new heights

and become famous for changing your industry . . . and, maybe, the world.

Having looked at all ten different routes to becoming an 80/20 manager, it's now time to see how they all fit together.

Executive Summary: The Complete 80/20 Manager

If you want a quality, act as if you already had it.

William James[1]

One shining quality lends a lustre to another, or hides a glaring defect.

William Hazlitt

The 80/20 manager can be all the things I've discussed in this book – investigating, superconnecting, mentoring, leveraging, liberating, seeking meaning, time-rich, simplifying, lazy and strategic. But I've never met a manager who fully embodies all of these traits. Inevitably, you will be more naturally inclined to some of these desiderata than others. Personally, after years of trying, I still don't score very high on laziness or mentoring. As always with the Principle, it might be better to make your strengths even more exceptional and not worry too much about correcting your weaknesses. We should view the ten qualities as different ways to become an 80/20 manager, rather than demand expertise in all of them. Becoming the best possible manager with respect to just one of the dimensions will still transform your work and career.

Yet, none of the qualities is unimportant for managerial super-effectiveness. Mastering each quality might be a short-term challenge, but the long-term benefits are so disproportionate that the effort you invest will be repaid tens or hundreds of times over the course of your career.

Managerial Attribute	Short-term Challenge	Long-term Benefit
Investigating	Low	High
Superconnecting	Low	High
Mentoring	Low	High
Leveraged	Low to Moderate	High
Liberating	Moderate	Very High
Seeking Meaning	Moderate	Enormous
Time-Rich	Moderate to High	Very High
Simplifying	Moderate to High	Very High
Lazy	High	Enormous
Strategic	High	Enormous

Let's recap the main aspects of each of the ten ways.

Investigating

- Children and detectives aside, few people spend their lives asking questions. But managers should.
- The world is not as it appears. Everyone focuses on averages, but business is driven forward by extremes. Beneath every average there are a few terrific forces and a mass of mediocre or bad ones. The trick is to work out which is which.
- A few questions are always worth asking. For instance:

1. Are a few products or customers super-profitable? (The answer is yes.)
2. What powerful idea could turbo-charge my business and my career?
3. Who is achieving great results, and how?
4. How can I do something important ten or twenty times better?
5. How can I get much more with much less?
6. Who is my most important customer?
7. Which single thing is holding me back more than anything else?

Superconnecting

- Turning points in our lives are rare. Oddly, they often come from people in the backgrounds of our lives, or even from those whose very existence we have forgotten.

- In the lottery of life, we can acquire, at high cost, a few 'red tickets' – qualifications, long experience and hard work. But we can also obtain an almost infinite number of low-cost 'green tickets' – weak links to people who move in different circles to our own. Any one of the green tickets could provide information that moves your life up a gear.
- The greatest benefit comes from and goes to the people who regularly put two of their contacts in touch with each other. These 'superconnectors' naturally stand at the junctions of novel ideas and fresh opportunities.
- We live in a 'small world' because superconnectors link disparate domains. Superconnectors are few in number but immensely influential and beneficial to society.
- It's easy to become a superconnecting manager, and the rewards are out of all proportion to the effort required.

Mentoring

- The former bosses you remember with affection are invariably those who taught you something. They were mentoring managers.
- Mentoring managers are open about their mistakes as well as their successes.
- Everyone needs encouragement and guidance. It's impossible to perform well without them.

- Many people believe mentoring is a big deal. It is in terms of results, but it isn't in terms of the time and energy needed. A few minutes each week, at the right time and with the right words to the right person, can make a world of difference. You can have a massive impact through very little effort.
- Watch for the small signals colleagues send out, indicating when they need support.
- Catch people doing something right and praise it wholeheartedly.
- Use the ten ways to help your people achieve greater results.
- Start a mentoring pyramid – insist that each member of staff you mentor mentors two of their colleagues.
- When seeking mentoring yourself, approach the person you really want, listen well to what they have to say, ask for help only when you truly need it, don't demand too much of their time, and give something back.
- Mentoring is most effective when it's enjoyable.

Leveraged

- When we really care about what we want to achieve, our subconscious mind works overtime to supply the answer.
- Visualize success. If you can't do that in your present job, find a setting where you feel more confident.
- Achieve success in your industry by recycling and

combining ideas that have worked wonders in other contexts.

- Reduce the number of decisions you make by at least 90 per cent, but increase the time you spend making vital decisions.
- Lack of trust leads to horrendous inefficiency, whereas a trusting environment enables much more to be done quickly and pleasurably.
- Hire and work exclusively with (and for) 'A' people. Make no exceptions.
- Maximize your use of the firm's capital. If a project promises exceptional returns, make the investment as big as possible. Entrepreneurs face greater risk, higher costs and a loss of control when they increase their capital investment. That is rarely true for managers.

Liberating

- In 1960, Douglas McGregor observed that there were two different ways of managing. Theory X relied on command and control, on the assumption that people would not work unless they were closely supervised or motivated by money. Theory Y assumed that people were motivated by curiosity, the wish to collaborate, and pleasure in their own skills.
- In any business activity where creativity is at all important, Theory Y is the '20 per cent solution' that delivers more than 80 per cent of the results.

- Yet many firms – even successful ones in exciting industries – still adhere to Theory X.
- It is virtually impossible to be a Theory Y manager in a Theory X firm, so don't even try.
- It requires an effort of will to liberate rather than control your team. Being a liberating manager is not a soft and squidgy option. It demands total honesty and openness, and the enforcement of high standards, but it is hugely rewarding.

Seeking meaning

- We find meaning in life and work through fulfilling our potential.
- Management is a creative calling, full of scope for idiosyncratic interpretation.
- In business, one person can have hundreds of times more impact than the average person. Breakthroughs come from a very small minority of ideas, enterprises, products, processes, customers and individuals. In this context, the Principle is more like 99/1 than 80/20.
- Individual inspiration and innovation are extremely scarce and valuable resources. Real, worthwhile success rests on unique attainments that have value to many other people.
- Meaning, too, is subject to the Principle. The few people who find true meaning in their work fuel progress for the world as a whole.

Time-rich

- For millennia, time and output were shackled together. Now that hobbling link has been smashed. Valuable output is not constraincd by, or measured in, man-hours.
- Experiments have proved that more leisure increases professional value. Fewer hours equals better results. Yet most managers don't act as if this is true. They still work long hours even though this has a negative impact on their output.
- If the 80/20 benchmark applies, we could work a two-day week and achieve 60 per cent more than when working a five-day week. But for senior managerial jobs, and any creative activity, that is a gross underestimate. A few crucial actions or decisions each week, month or even year may add 99 per cent (or more) of the value in 1 per cent (or less) of the time.
- Systematic examination of how managers work shows that most of them muddle through. They *like* interruptions and crises. It's hard to resist distractions and work only on vital matters, so very few managers do it.
- It takes discipline and non-conformity to buck the trend, but doing so leads to dramatically better results at work and in life.

Simplifying

- The most successful managers have a knack of taking a complex picture and rendering its essence in a simple, graphic and memorable way.
- Most managers love complexity, so simplifying is hard because it goes against the managerial grain. However, it becomes a lot easier once we acknowledge and take steps to correct our natural tendency to overcomplicate.
- Avoid problems that cannot be simplified. Concentrate, instead, on a few important issues where simplification is possible and will yield powerful results.
- Solutions do not require understanding of all the causes of business riddles. Even if we're not sure we have the right simple solution, we can experiment.
- The greatest challenge for any business based on product innovation is how to simplify its products and in the process make them more affordable and easier to use. Product simplification is hard to achieve but it is a sure route to market domination and expansion.
- Start each week and each day with one simple objective.
- Simplifying is the manager's most neglected art. It opens the door to solving previously intractable problems, enabling the team to surmount them. To simplify is to lead.

Lazy

- Laziness is the road to progress, but only when it is allied to intelligent thought and high ambition.
- Lazy, intelligent managers make the best bosses and CEOs.
- Laziness enforces selectivity, and success requires selectivity. We achieve most when we have the time and leisure to focus on the big breaks and big decisions.
- All successful business careers flow from a few critical decisions, made infrequently.
- Inherent laziness is nothing to admire. The best lazy managers have acquired their laziness by working at it for years.

Strategic

- Strategic managers dream up dramatically better ways of doing business in their respective industries.
- They think, they devise a superior business model and a strategy to achieve it, and they have the determination and courage to make it a reality.
- Managers who have reconstructed their industries often:
  - o bring a new type of person into the industry;
  - o vastly increase collaboration;
  - o invent a new model that slashes costs and fattens margins;

o appeal to customers in a novel way; and/or
o make themselves the brand, and the model for the organization.

What unites all the ways to be an 80/20 manager?

In reducing the 80/20 manager to a set of qualities and actions, there is a danger of missing the big picture, of overcomplicating something really simple and forceful. The essence of the 80/20 manager is a driven concern for results, and respect for life's lopsided pattern of achieving them.

Being an 80/20 manager means thinking, each day: What *big* goal can I achieve with relatively *little* effort? Both components – the ambition and the ease – are essential for results-based living and working. Managers who work too hard and miss the forest for the trees will not achieve great success. Nor will managers who have modest aspirations.

If we can't achieve good results through reasonable effort, it's impossible to achieve great results from trying harder. Often we need to try less or even give up before we can achieve something wonderful. This doesn't mean trying something inferior, just something different and, ideally superior; or finding a different way to approach the same goal. It's not that everything should be effortless, but each 80/20 manager should spend their time on something that they can do *much better* and *more easily* than any of their colleagues. And it's even better if the manager can do that particular thing better and more easily than anyone else in the world. Yet it often takes years, even a lifetime, to discover what that thing is.

The sure way never to find your power alley is to try harder at something you are not doing particularly well now.

Instead, think:

What worthwhile result – the bigger the better – could I achieve to a higher degree, and through less effort, than anybody else? This mode of thought will inevitably involve drawing on your unique knowledge, imagination and willpower. You must passionately want to hit the desired target and you must know a trick or two that will enable you to do so faster, more accurately and with less sweat than anyone else.

But 80/20 managers also know how to limit their own personal input, and how to draw on help from outside. Achieving goals is never a solo effort – other people's ideas, hard work, dedication and sometimes money will be needed. If you try to do too much on your own, you will fail or compromise the integrity of your ideal.

In the Western world, our ingrained Protestant work ethic may tell us that the Principle sounds like a justification for a small elite to enjoy a wonderful life while the mass of workers toils away in the salt mines. But in this context, our ethics are leading us astray. In an ideal 80/20 world, *everyone* would work where they could achieve the most, where they could get the best results in the least time and with the least stress.

A huge number of activities sap time, goodwill and

resources in business and wider society, including clocking-in, pointless meetings, irksome supervision, serving the wrong customers, forcing children and adults to obey arbitrary orders, seeking status, violence and war. Theory X managers – and those they manage – view all of these as essential. Theory Y managers understand the importance of avoiding them. By definition, liberating managers do less themselves – they liberate; they do not control; and the action goes on when they are not present and even after they are long dead.

80/20 managers will always be a minority. Even if the general level of management skill increases significantly from today's level, as it has in the past and probably will in the future, they will remain exceptional, whatever norm is prevailing. The world will never be full of 80/20 managers, because the Principle cannot allow that to happen. But I trust that a few more 80/20 managers – perhaps even a few million more – will emerge and help to create a world that is far more comfortable and fascinating, and richer in every way, than the one with which we are familiar.

And why shouldn't you be one of those new 80/20 managers?

Finale: The 80/20 Manager and the 80/20 Organization

And God created the Organization and
gave It dominion over man.
> Robert Townsend[1], Genesis 1, 30A,
> Subparagraph VIII

There are fifty ways to leave your lover, but
only six exits from this airplane.
> Southwest Airlines safety announcement

80/20 managers need 80/20 organizations, just as 80/20 organizations need 80/20 managers.

80/20 companies possess proprietary knowledge and earn high returns, mainly from 'star businesses' – leadership positions in high-growth markets. They are innovators that have reinvented their markets. A corporation that is growing fast and is sustainably profitable is an 80/20 company, even if none of its managers has heard of the Principle. It doesn't matter if a company appreciates or announces that it is an 80/20 firm, as long as it behaves like one – as long as it innovates, grows fast, enjoys high margins and liberates the talents of its people. As Shakespeare almost said, a dog by any other name would bark as well.

But might we see the emergence of a new type of self-consciously 80/20 company, one that uses the Principle to reinforce and extend its edge? Like an 80/20 manager, a 'super 80/20 company' would have highly selective strategies. It would:

- Carefully identify the company's core – the compound of the firm's personality and DNA, its way of competing (operational excellence, product leadership and/or customer intimacy), its core resources, its core customers and why they like the company, and its core products and processes – then devote all its energy to deepening the core, making it daily more impressive, attractive and totally different from anything offered by a rival.
- Liberate its employees, and require that everyone behaves openly and honestly with their colleagues.
- Identify the small parts of its customer base that account for most or all (or more than all) its true value.
- Focus internal energy on nurturing these customers, gaining 100 per cent of their relevant business, selling more to them and devising new products

that can be sold to the core customers at high margins.

- Prospect for new customers who are similar to the existing super-profitable ones, both in existing geographies and beyond.
- Make unprofitable customers profitable by raising prices and lowering the costs of recruiting and serving them; or, if this is not possible, lose them.
- Focus on the few product lines and businesses that account for most or all (or more than all) its true value, expand their sales and develop extensions.
- Simplify the core products, because making them more affordable and intelligible will open up vast new markets.
- Create wonderful new, simple products by making full use of the firm's unique characteristics and creativity.
- Make unprofitable products profitable by raising prices and lowering costs; or, if this is impossible, run to generate cash, or, if this is also impossible, stop making them.
- Sell any business that proves unable to make high returns, unless it is necessary to serve core customers.
- Inspire every employee to make the firm's core deeper and more powerful.
- Hammer out its strategy in one sentence, and ensure that everyone in the firm knows what that strategy is and how they can advance it every day.

While liberating its people, the 'super 80/20 company' would also stretch them by:

- Turning them into 80/20 managers, multiplying their clout while ensuring that they have plenty of free time to think, enjoy work and life, and fulfil their family and social obligations.
- Hiring only 80/20 managers or those who will quickly become one. Being an 80/20 manager involves respecting all employees, helping them to become more skilful and creative, and behaving with warmth, authenticity and integrity.
- Encouraging executives who cannot or will not become 80/20 managers to leave.
- Running 80/20 workshops, sharing the best examples of 80/20 analyses and practices.
- Developing mentoring programmes to reinforce and extend 80/20 learning.
- Building 80/20 project teams, which will be small, cohesive, agile, quick to attain their single purpose, and quick to disband.
- Establishing weak links to contrasting teams and individuals outside the firm.
- 'Twinning' with another 80/20 company in a different industry or country to share knowledge and insights.

Yet, it is not always advisable for an 80/20 manager to remain in a 'super 80/20 company'. Once their imagination and horizons have been extended, they may spot new opportunities that they can pursue better outside the firm. The most transformational firms are, paradoxically, often the best ones to leave. Leaders cannot stimulate excellence and innovative thinking, yet corral it within the firm's walls. Nor should they. A true 80/20 firm has strength in depth, so it will probably continue to thrive despite the periodic loss of many excellent managers. It might even benefit from forming new relationships with them after they leave. But even if departures do leave holes that cannot be filled, the founding of great new firms is more important to the economy and wider society than the preservation of great existing firms. For that reason, 80/20 managers should always be mobile.

Some successful firms find this hard to accept. They foster a cult that exalts the company and denigrates any defectors. But this is hypocritical. Either you believe in individual development and self-expression, wherever it leads, or you do not. The best leaders openly encourage their people to take control of their careers, and then maintain lifelong friendly relationships with their former protégés. They appreciate that there is no shortage of talent; there is only a shortage of firms that are prepared to liberate it. Ultimately, the individual is more important than the family, the company or the state. The best families, companies and states all recognize this.

Greatness is collective, but its foundation is individual and ever-shifting. Liberating greatness within yourself and then within your colleagues might seem to need a miracle, but it's easy once you know how. The secret to being an

80/20 manager is to realize sky-high aspirations through intelligence and acute observation instead of through toil and trouble. Like angels, we can soar and lift humanity while scarcely flapping our wings. But unless we care deeply about specific results, and unless our ambition is boundless, we will never even take off.

Notes

Part One

Chapter One

1. Peter James (2009) *Dead Tomorrow*, London: Macmillan, page 49.
2. Robert Townsend (1970) *Up the Organization: How to Stop the Corporation from Stifling People and Strangling Profits*, London: Michael Joseph, page 9. (A new edition was published by Jossey-Bass in 2007).
3. Ibid., pages 10 and 107.

Chapter Two

1. Quoted in Walter Isaacson (2011) *Steve Jobs*, London: Little Brown, page 78. The 'Marketing Philosophy' was written by Mike Markkula shortly after the Apple computer Co. was officially incorporated.
2. Ibid. In the 'Marketing Philosophy', 'focus' is the second of three points. The other two are 'empathy' (with the customer) and 'impute', meaning the impression people gain of a company or product from the signals it conveys.
3. Ibid., page 337.
4. 'Apple's Strategy with Final Cut Pro X', http:macintopics.com/2011/09/31/apple/final-cut-pro/apples-strategy-with-final-cut-pro-x, 31 August 2011, retrieved 23 January 2012.

5. Isaacson, op.cit., page 466.
6. Isaacson, op.cit., page 474.
7. Sales of the iPhone: 'iPhone', Wikipedia, retrieved 2 February 2012; iPhone profits compared to all cellphone sales: Isaacson, op. cit., page 474.
8. 'Breaking Bin Laden: Visualizing the Power of a Single Tweet', socialflow.com, 6 May 2011, http://blog.socialflow.com/post/5246404319/breaking-bin-laden-visualizing-the-power-of-a-single, retrieved 28 September 2012.
9. Silicon Valley Insider, 31 March 2011 and the author's analysis. Assumptions are that those following between 2 and 50 people followed 10, on average; that those following between 51 and 500 people followed 150, on average; and that those following between 501 and 524,000 people followed 1000, on average. The calculation doesn't change very much if you make different assumptions. Note that at the time of writing (October 2012), the number of registered Twitter users had increased to more than half a billion, but the shape of the graph remains exactly the same when the figures are amended to take this into account.
10. Nielsen BookScan data, retrieved 24 March 2011.
11. Nielsen BookScan data, retrieved 17 October 2012.
12. Data from the Census of 21 April 1991, retrieved from the website http://www.citypopulation.de.
13. Shaomei Wu, Jake M. Hofman, Winter A. Mason and Duncan J. Watts (2011) 'Who Says What to Whom on Twitter', Yahoo! Research, http://research.yahoo.com/node/3386, retrieved 28 September 2012.
14. Nassim N. Taleb, Daniel G. Goldstein and Mark W. Spitznagel (2009) 'The Six Mistakes Executives Make in Risk Management', *Harvard Business Review*, October, page 79.
15. 'The Wealth Gap – Inequality in Numbers', 17 January 2012, http://www.bbc.co.uk/news/business-1654898, pages 1–2.
16. Niall Ferguson (2011) *Civilization: The West and the Rest*, London: Allen Lane, page 235.
17. *New York Times*, 21 June 1999. The researchers were Bernado Huberman and Lada Adamic.

18. 'Chaos Theory Explodes Hollywood Hype', *Independent on Sunday* (London), 30 March 1997.
19. Bill Bryson (2010) *At Home: A Short History of Private Life*, London: Doubleday, pages 41–2. The other five plants are cassava, sorghum, millet, rye and oats.
20. David Baldacci (2010) *Deliver Us From Evil*, New York: Hachette, page 416.
21. Chris Anderson (2006) *The Long Tail: Why the Future of Business is Selling Less of More*, New York: Random House.
22. Anita Elberse (2008) 'Should You Invest in the Long Tail?', *Harvard Business Review*, July–August, pages 88–96. The quotation is from page 92.
23. Ibid., page 92.
24. Interview with Eric Schmidt for McKinsey Quarterly, September 2008.
25. Richard Koch (2004) *Living the 80/20 Way: Work Less, Worry Less, Succeed More, Enjoy More*, London: Nicholas Brealey, page 13.

Part Two

Way One: The Investigating Manager

1. David J. Collis and Cynthia A. Montgomery (2008) 'Competing on Resources', *Harvard Business Review*, July–August, pages 140–50.

Way Two: The Superconnecting Manager

1. Mark S. Granovetter (1973) 'The Strength of Weak Ties', *American Journal of Sociology* 78 (6) (May), pages 1360–80.
2. Quoted in Isaacson, op. cit., page 431.
3. Granovetter, op. cit.
4. Ibid.
5. Jeffrey Travers and Stanley Milgram (1969) 'An Experimental Study of the Small World Problem', *Society* 39 (2), pages 61–6.
6. Quoted in Stanley Milgram, 'The Small World Problem', *Psychology Today* issue 1, 1967, pages 61–7.

7. I have co-authored a book about the power of superconnectors and the strength of weak links: see Richard Koch and Greg Lockwood (2010) *Superconnect*, London: Little, Brown; New York: W.W. Norton & Company.

Way Three: The Mentoring Manager
1. Jack Canfield with Janet Switzer (2005) *The Success Principles: How to Get From Where You Are to Where You Want to Be*, New York: HarperCollins.
2. Many thanks to Matthew Kelly for contributing this story to the book.
3. Canfield, op.cit.

Way Four: The Leveraged Manager
1. Ap Dijksterhuis and Loren F. Nordren (2006) 'A Theory of Unconscious Thought', *Perspectives on Psychological Science* 1 (2), pages 95–109.
2. Isaacson, op. cit., page 100.

Way Five: The Liberating Manager
1. Personal Interview, 29 March 2011.
2. Benjamin Franklin (1758) 'Preface', in *Poor Richard's Almanack*, reprinted as a separate book (1986) *The Way to Wealth*, Bedford, MA: Applewood Books, page 17.

Way Six: The Manager Seeking Meaning
1. Joseph Conrad (1902, 2007) *Heart of Darkness*, London: Penguin.
2. Victor E. Frankel (1959, 2006) *Man's Search for Meaning*, Boston: Beacon Press.
3. http://www.brainyquote.com/quotes/quotes/b/bertrandru378106.html
4. Charles Taylor (1989) *Sources of the Self: The Making of the Modern Identity*, Cambridge: Cambridge University Press, page 375.
5. William H. Whyte (1956) *The Organization Man*, New York: Simon and Schuster.

6. The manager, Whyte said in conclusion, 'must *fight* The Organization. Not stupidly, or selfishly . . . But fight he must, for the demands for his surrender are constant and powerful . . . the peace of mind offered by The Organization remains a surrender, and no less so for being offered in benevolence. That is the problem.' Ibid., page 372.

7. Peter F. Drucker (1995) *Managing in a Time of Great Change*, London: Butterworth-Heinemann. The quotation is from the essay 'A Century of Social Transformation', chapter 21 of the book.

8. Andrew S. Grove (1998) *Only the Paranoid Survive*, London: Profile Books.

9. Richard K. Lochridge (1981) 'Specialization', in Carl W. Stern and George Stalk Jr. (eds) (1998) *Perspectives on Strategy from The Boston Consulting Group*, New York: John Wiley.

10. The average internal rate of return was 113 per cent on realised investments (Bain Capital prospectus and author's personal experience).

Way Seven: The Time-Rich Manager

1. Marshall McLuhan (1964, 1993) *Understanding Media: The Extensions of Man*, London: Routledge.

2. Manuel Castells (1996) *The Rise of the Network Society* (Volume 1 of *The Information Age: Economy, Society and Culture*), Massachusetts: Blackwell, page 467 (note 78).

3. Quoted in James B. Stewart (2005) *DisneyWar: The Battle for the Magic Kingdom*, New York: Simon and Schuster.

4. Franklin, op. cit., pages 11, 12, and 16.

5. Ibid., page 17.

6. Stewart, op. cit.

7. Graham Robb (2007) *The Discovery of France*, New York: W.W. Norton.

8. Jeremy Rifkin (1995, 2004) *The End of Work: The Decline of the Global Labor Force and the Dawn of the Post-Market Era*, New York: Putnam.

9. Ibid., pages 304–7. For example, in the United States, managers,

professionals and technicians comprised 22.9 per cent of the workforce in 1960, but this had risen to 29.7 per cent by 1990. In the UK, the increase was even more dramatic – from 11.4 per cent in 1961 to 32.8 per cent in 1990. In Japan, the trend was similar but not so pronounced – from 6.8 per cent in 1955 to 14.9 per cent in 1990.

10. http://www.bbc.co.uk/news/magazine-17155304, retrieved 22 March 2012.

11. Henry Mintzberg (1973) *The Nature of Managerial Work*, New York: Harper and Row.

12. Leslie A. Perlow and Jessica L. Porter (2009) 'Making Time Off Predictable and Required', *Harvard Business Review*, October, pages 102–9.

13. Elliott Jaques (1961) *Equitable Payment: A General Theory of Work, Differential Payment, and Individual Progress*, London: Heinemann.

14. An updated version of the book is still in print: C. Northcote Parkinson (1958, 1981) *The Law*, Harmondsworth: Penguin.

Way Eight: The Simplifying Manager

1. Isaacson, op. cit., page 126.

2. David Brooks (2011) *The Social Animal*, New York: Random House, page 338.

3. Quoted in Ken Favaro, Per Ola Karlsson and Gary L. Neilson (2011) 'The Four Types of CEOs', *strategy+business*, 63, page 45.

4. The research is by Professor Claudio Del Percio of Sapienza University, Rome. Mentioned in Brooks, op. cit., page 130.

5. M. Scott Peck (1981, 1990) *The Road Less Travelled: A New Psychology of Love, Traditional Values and Spiritual Growth*, London: Arrow Books. (A more recent (2008) edition is also available from Rider.)

6. Oscar Wilde (1895) *The Importance of Being Earnest*, act 1.

7. Quoted in Carl W. Stern and George Stalk Jr. (eds) (1998) *Perspectives on Strategy from The Boston Consulting Group*, New York: John Wiley, page xiv.

8. Isaacson, op. cit., page 101.
9. Ibid., page 80.
10. Ibid., page 73.
11. Ibid., page 95.
12. Ibid., page 97.
13. Ibid., page 99.
14. Ibid., page 491.
15. Ibid., page 123.
16. Warren Buffett (2010) 'Letter to Shareholders', in Annual Report of Berkshire Hathaway Inc.

Way Nine: The Lazy Manager

1. John Ruskin (1851, 1903) *The Works of John Ruskin*, edited by E. T. Cook and Alexander Wedderburn, volume 12, Pre-Raphaelitism, London: George Allen.
2. Interview in the *Guardian*, 31 March 1987.
3. Quoted in Liz Roman Gallese (1989) 'Counsellor to the King', *New York Times*, 24 September 1989.
4. Bertrand Russell (1932) 'In Praise of Idleness', http://grammar.about.com/od/classicessays/a/praiseidleness.htm, retrieved 10 October 2012.
5. Erich Von Manstein (1955) *Verlorene Seige*, translated into English as *Lost Victories* (1958, 2004), edited by Anthony G. Powell St Paul, MN: Zenith.
6. Bertrand Russell (1932), op. cit.
7. Christopher Morley (1920) 'On Laziness', http://grammar.about.com/od/classicessays/a/onlazinessessay.htm, retrieved 10 October 2012.
8. Quoted in Richard Koch (2005) *The Breakthrough Principle of 16X*, Dallas: Pritchett, page 17.

Way Ten: The Strategic Manager

1. Google mission statement – from Google Corporate Information, www.google.com/about/company, retrieved 19 October 2012.

Executive Summary: The Complete 80/20 Manager
1. http://thinkexist.com/quotation/if_you_want_a_quality_act_as_
if_you_already_had/226772.html

Finale: The 80/20 Manager and the 80/20 Organization
1. Townsend, op. cit., page 7.

Index

Numbers in bold refer to diagrams.